Transparently
BEHIND THE SCENES OF A GOOD LIFE

Sarah,

So great to meet in Person!

(My life is an open book)

Lisa Salazar

Nov. 11, 2017

Lisa Salazar

ISBN-13: 978-0986931901
ISBN-10: 098693190X
eBook ISBN: 978-1-61914-492-7

transparently.ca
contact@transparently.ca

Cover and book design by Lisa Salazar.

Table of Contents

Foreword by Duncan Holmes   1

Foreword by kaitlyn Bogas   6

Preface   8

Chapter 1: Trip to the Moon   11

Chapter 2: California, Here We Come   16

Chapter 3: Growing Roots   21

Chapter 4: A New Awareness   25

Chapter 5: How American   32

Chapter 6: A Sticky Situation   37

Chapter 7: On the Meaning of Words   42

Chapter 8: The Power of Advertising   47

Chapter 9: The Big Bust   51

Chapter 10: What Do I Know?   56

Chapter 11: Spiritual War   61

Chapter 12: Stupid Zeal   65

Chapter 13: We Meet Again   72

Chapter 14: Fundamentally Speaking   77

Chapter 15: Crossing the Border   81

Chapter 16: Homesickness or Love?   89

Chapter 17: The Countdown   95

Chapter 18: I Promise   100

Chapter 19: Starting a Family   105

Chapter 20: Full of Beans & Fessing Up   111

Chapter 21: Hitting Rock Bottom   119

Chapter 22: Fear of Falling   127

Chapter 23: Cocoon Time   131

Chapter 24: Gender Clinic   136

Chapter 25: A Disaster and a Wedding   142

Chapter 26: What Will People Think?   147

Chapter 27: The Day the Music Stopped   153

Chapter 28: Hormones   163

Chapter 29: The Last Hurdles   168

Chapter 30: Running Into Transition   175

Chapter 31: Navigating Uncharted Waters   181

Chapter 32: The Change   192

Chapter 33: An Epilogue   199

The Last Word: 202

Appendix I: Bed Posts   203

Appendix II: The Letter   208

Where did the name "Lisa" come from?   213

Foreword by Duncan Holmes

When I first met Santiago Salazar and his brother Enrique, they almost seemed like conjoined twins. That wasn't the case, of course, because while it seemed they worked with a common, complementary creative brain, and occasionally finished each other's sentences, Enrique was older than Santiago, and, as I got to know them better, I discovered there were substantial differences in their personalities, in the way they did things, went about their lives—and how those lives would unfold.

Enrique and Santiago—we Anglicized the Spanish and called him Jim—were brothers who had put their wildly artistic talents together to form Salazar Graphics, a hot little firm that, with others in town, supported Vancouver's ad agency business in the Mad Men days of the Sixties, and on into the more docile decades that followed. Salazar Graphics worked out of offices in the city's historic Gastown district, then in a period of rebirth. Along with cosmetic change that brought old bricks back to life, Gastown became a gathering place for tie-dyed, flower-power kids, and endless stores that were hung with psychedelic black light posters of the era—all embalmed in stupefying clouds of patchouli and pot that sold for fifteen bucks a lid.

Your conclusion about now may be that the brothers Salazar, in the middle of all of this peace and love, worked stoned out of their minds from dawn until dusk. Actually, quite the opposite. As I observed them, in surroundings that attracted, tempted and convinced others to take dope-filled paths to blissful nirvana, these Colombian-born, California-schooled kids were as straight as dies. Enrique may have knocked back an occasional doobie or double scotch, but I'm sure that Santiago held fast to a disciplined straight and narrow, and unknowingly—or not!—influenced his brother to be more like him, and hold Satan at bay. I simply don't know. All I know is that I was in awe of their work, and knew little of their personal 'scene,' because at that stage my relationship involved their talent and not their personal time. They hinted at quiet, Christian, family-oriented lives. I, meanwhile, was front and centre in a crazy party of life, and the Salazars had chosen another venue.

I met Enrique and Santiago when I became marketing director for the new and burgeoning Keg Restaurants family. With ease, and direction that seemed to come from their very hearts, they were able to chart a graphics course for the Keg in its early, rapidly-growing years. Again, the skills of one complemented the talents of the other. Not only were their images right, but the execution of the art was magnificent. Every piece, from typography to illustration, reflected superb training, a desire to take ever-bigger creative steps, to make things work the way they should.

I must say that as our relationship grew, I too seemed to become creatively one with both of them. It was very satisfying, even as these quiet, unassuming Colombians continued to remain on the extreme edges—if at all—of what became famously and infamously known as Keg Good Times.

Over the years, as we saw more of each other with Keg, and later with other clients, I learned more of the Salazars, even if we never really became social partners. As Enrique continued his bachelor life, Jim shared his family stories as I shared mine. His wife and three sons. My wife and four daughters. I met his siblings and his parents, who I always figured looked the part of comfortable Colombians, continuing always to converse in Spanish with their sons—as close knit as a family could ever be. And as with Jim, I suspected that their Christian faith too was strong, even if this course of personal belief never seemed to manifest itself in too much joy. My inclination on many occasions was to question why melancholy seemed to pervade their collective lives. I never asked.

I can't recall exactly when these events happened, but somewhere in our relationship there were two shockers. Out of the blue one day, Enrique blacked out and slammed into a parked car. He was diagnosed with brain cancer, and after a prolonged downhill ride, a man who in retrospect I barely knew, left us. It was a huge gap in this close-knit family, the loss for me of a friend. The second thing? Jim confided in me the details of a great life secret. As a child in California, he had been coaxed into a private setting and sexually molested by someone he believed he could trust.

I can't explain why, but it was difficult for me to understand how this incident had so affected him. As a child, for some inexplicable reason, I blackmailed the man involved in a similar sexual encounter, demanding money or exposure of his crime. Then I promptly thought no more about it. Judge me, as you will.

Jim's admission opened a door to deeper exchanges between us, and in the years that followed we shared much, even as I believe, I sought more. My journalistic curiosity prompted an ongoing need to keep prying about Jim's life, the secrets that perhaps remained to be shared?

On Friday, October 15, 2007, again out of the blue, there was a much bigger message, that opened Santiago Salazar's life book in a spectacular way. On the previous Friday afternoon, answering a question about what he was up to, Jim said he was working on a biographical thing—about himself. I said that when it was done I would love to read it, and he said when it was finished, that maybe I could. On the Monday, after discussing an unrelated client thing, I asked about the progress of the bio, and could I read it? Jim hesitated, but agreed, on condition that it be read jointly by me and partner Joyce.

I can't remember exactly how Jim's Big Message was first broached, but he said his life was about to change, and could I guess how? To me it seemed obvious. He would enter the ministry. This was a guy who could quote the bible chapter and verse, who spent regular mornings in its study, who was a disciplined churchgoer and Sunday in-church performer. It seemed quite logical that in this light-bulb moment he would chuck commercial art for the ecclesiastical cloth.

No, he said, not that.

It was a long e-mail—almost as long as my words to date. It told of a life of pain, a life where something physical, physiological, emotional and more had been trapped inside his body. Inside him was a woman. And the time had come to free her. Santiago, Jim would become Lisa.

My immediate reaction, regardless of the huge consequences that I knew would be forthcoming in Lisa's life, was joy. Joy that this imprisoned person could break out and take a natural path to potential happiness. This, I said to myself, had been the reason for all of those years of sadness. A butterfly in whatever form would emerge awkwardly from a chrysalis and fly into an endless life of sunshine. Saints be praised!

Jim would later say: "Our short conversation (on Monday) and the subsequent one ten minutes later when you called back became forever cast in my memory. My life didn't come to an end as I had feared. Instead, your words that day helped cut an opening for the path that would widen with time. I am so grateful to you and Joyce...

"I will never forget the comment you made when you called me after reading the letter. You said that this explained why every time you walked away from one of those heavy conversations that you wondered to yourself what made me so incredibly sad. You admitted how you had tried to pry open that very private door on more than one occasion, to which I replied that I sensed that—and would try to change the subject or deflect you away."

And no, Lisa said later, the earlier sexual encounter had not caused the dysphoria. It only added to (Jim's) deep confusion and self loathing. I understood.

In the subsequent year, as the Santiago of yesterday disappeared quietly into the grey blur of history, we watched Lisa walk ever more confidently into a new world of womanhood. It was always a vision of pride, of bravery, and of new-found happiness.

One day, when she smiles as she dances, we will stand, misty eyed, to applaud.

Duncan Holmes — *Vancouver, BC*

Foreword by kaitlyn Bogas

I met Lisa in the fall of 2009. I had written an article about my own transition for a local Vancouver publication, and Lisa had responded online in support to what she had read. It was, as far as I know, the first time that she had really "outed" herself publicly. It was something that she really didn't have to do, and hadn't planned to do, but I am ever so glad that she did. On that day, Lisa took a huge step in becoming who she is today, a wonderful woman of love and compassion, who I'm quite certain will spend a lifetime helping others.

I'm not certain why many among us choose to make our stories public. Perhaps we are all too aware of the stigma that is attached to being trans, and wish so desperately for those around us to understand. We believe that it's all so logical, that everyone will just "get it" if we beat them over the head long enough, with our stories of personal liberation.

Perhaps, on the other hand, we just feel so much like celebrating that we made it through our tormented pasts, and survived long enough to reach transition, that we feel like shouting through the streets. It is indeed a perilous journey, fraught with frustration, lies, torment, and heartbreak. According to available statistics, nearly forty percent of transsexuals will choose to end their lives, rather than face the humiliation of society by transitioning.

Transitioning requires a tremendous leap of faith on the part of the individual. I believe that we must prepare ourselves to lose everything that we hold dear. Our spouses, children, mothers, fathers, sisters, brothers, business associates, friends, our jobs. Our very ability to take care of ourselves and our families is compromised the second you come out. And all of this for what, there's no pink, or blue light in your brain that shows up in a CT scan, no blood test, no genetic tests, no tattoo behind your left ear. All that you have is that persistent feeling that you are not who you appear to be, and yes, that thought never leaves.

I would ask of you then, that you share in this leap of faith that Lisa felt so compelled to follow. Open your mind to her story, she has no reason to lie to you. Accept what she has to tell you, the good, the bad, the confusing, the things that she has done that have hurt those people closest to her. Your understanding of her condition will help so many others, and help you to see the world for what it truly is, a place filled with both wonder, and confusion.

Keep compassion in your heart, and allow Lisa to take you through an amazing life story!

kaitlyn Bogas — *Vancouver BC*

Preface

Shortly after Christmas 2009, I began a correspondence with a friend who, in the course of a few emails, had asked me many probing questions. After several long email responses I said that, thanks to her questioning, I perhaps had a good start to a book. She said the more I answered her questions the more she wanted to know, and she encouraged me to keep going. It was now the end of February and, though I initially balked at the idea of writing a book about my life, something therapeutic going on as I recounted my stories. As I continued writing throughout the month of March, I laughed and cried to myself more than I ever had. I was surprised at how it all came together so quickly, especially since I had never written anything longer than a term paper—and that was way back in my college days.

As I thought about an appropriate title for this book, I considered all kinds of possibilities, but I also questioned my motivation for telling my story and whether anyone would bother reading it. What could I add that has not already been said by others; and what, if any thing, would the be differentiating quality of the book?

I didn't want to add yet another title to the growing number of books about the lives of transgender people. Least of all, I didn't want anybody reading this book expecting it to be a herald for "the cause." Additionally, I felt it needed to be stated right from the beginning that my life has not been a tragedy, and that I do not deserve or want pity or admiration. I can think of a hundred worse things than being transgender, and my "suffering"—if you want to call it that—pales by comparison to what others have to endure from the day they are born until the day they die.

Consequently, the title I picked is the most descriptive of what this book really is all about. It's a look behind the scenes of a good life and the process of becoming transparent about who I am. The truth is, though I lived with a secret identity crisis, I have also had a blessed, busy and happy life.

Dedicating this book to just one person was impossible for me to do. First of all, I have been blessed with amazing parents and siblings. But I am most grateful for and to the woman I married, to have been known as her husband and the father of her children. And I am most fortunate, because as well as having these people in my life, I have also been surrounded by an amazing collection of friends. I can honestly say on these facts alone that I have had a very good life. To all of you, my family and my friends, thank you for allowing me to have journeyed with you in the past, and for the amazing gift of allowing me to continue with you now.

Finally, I must acknowledge one person above all others, Jesus the Christ. I acknowledge Him because He is the thread running through the tapestry of my life in such an intricate way, it has kept the weave together and prevented it from unraveling.

If you want it put in a less religious way, okay: I have been kept from going nuts, harming myself (or worse) by a Higher Power.

Distraction from one's problems is a good thing, and this adventure—my life—has had an ample supply of distractions. But there has always been this very private and confusing tension behind the scenes that took me more than forty years to understand and another fifteen years to reconcile.

One last comment: These accounts deal with some sensitive issues that on today's television shows are usually preceded with the warning "adult content, viewer discretion is advised." If you are uncomfortable with the "adult" words for body parts and swear words, then be warned: I use them. I mean no offense or disrespect.

Chapter 1: Trip to the Moon

The flight that day from Bogotá to Miami via Panama City was un-eventful for the seasoned crew of the *Braniff Airlines* DC-7. But in the mind and reality of an almost ten-year-old taking his first trip on an airplane, it was a monumental experience—on a level of going to the moon. It was October 6, 1960, and my family had been planning this trip for close to two years. This was it. We were moving to the United States! We were five children ranging from two to sixteen years, with me smack in the middle. Add to that my mom, dad, and my grandmother—there were eight of us in all.

I still remember the commotion at El Dorado, Bogotá's inter-national airport the morning we left. My aunts, uncles, and all of our cousins and close family friends came to see us off. It was a huge en-tourage, with some crying and others cheering us on. I was numb from many mixed emotions. I was excited, but didn't know if I should be sad and crying, or cheerful and happy. Our family was the first of the extended family to migrate as a group, and it was hard to com-pletely appreciate the moment. Of all my first cousins—and there were many—only a few have remained in Colombia to this day. In the fifty years since we left, many also made their move to the U.S., and are now grand and great-grandparents, with their families scattered across Florida and Texas.

Moving to the United States was a coveted thing to do. I was in the fourth grade when we left, and the envy of my classmates. I was going to America! I was the luckiest person they knew. That we were planning to live in California gave my friends all the more reason to be jealous. It was too much for my mind to grasp. There was a much deeper aspect to this almost universal appeal for life in the United States, but at the time I had no idea what it might be.

I refer to the geopolitical climate of the time. Castro had succeeded in overthrowing Batista in Cuba. What if the leftist guerrillas operating in Colombia and other South American countries also succeeded? This may have contributed to my parent's desire to affect a change. But there were other reasons, which I will elaborate on later.

I envisioned California as a big Disneyland, with sunny beaches, blue jeans and Milky Way candy bars—images forged in my mind from movies, the *Wonderful World of Disney* that aired every Sunday night on Bogotá's one television station, and the stories from those who had gone to "paradise" and returned wearing Levis and chomping on chocolate bars and Bazooka bubble gum.

Bogotá's climate is fairly constant all year round, being so close to the Equator. And being so high in the Andes, its temperatures are very mild, warm during the day and cool at night—strikingly different from the climate in Florida on the day we arrived. The first blast of air to hit us as we exited the airplane on the tarmac in Miami was hot and muggy, with the smell of diesel fuel mixed with a noticeable humid muskiness that lasted until we entered the air-conditioned terminal.

We had a mountain of suitcases with us, and it took us ages to clear immigration and customs. Only my father and older sister could speak English. My dad would take turns with my mom holding my baby brother, while the rest of us waited quietly as my dad dealt with the officials, and presented all our customs declarations, visas and passports.

We landed with what my mom felt we would need to survive our first month in the U.S. My parents had sold off many of our belongings in a couple of garage sales that were organized by a *gringa* who had experience in such matters. Some of the larger things were put in storage in case we returned after a few years, and the rest was shipped through the Panama Canal to San Francisco.

We had only lived three years in our new house, which sat on two large lots in a new suburb in the north of Bogotá. One half of the property was yard, and my dad, who along with my mom was a golf enthusiast, placed a very short par three hole on it, complete with green and bunkers. The house had marble floors and huge plate glass windows, which ran the whole length of the house facing the yard. (Dad and my uncles owned a marble mill and contracting company; this explains the marble floors. Dad was the firm's administrator; his two oldest brothers were both civil engineers and the founding senior partners.)

My parents chose not to sell the house in Bogotá, since they wanted to keep the door open in case we returned to Colombia. Instead, the house was leased to the American Embassy for a U.S. Air Force colonel, part of the American mission in Colombia. The lease was for three years; this set the timer for our possible return.

For our first two weeks in the U.S. we stayed at the Golden Nugget Motel in Miami Beach. It was perhaps the longest vacation we had ever taken as a family. We kids spent much of our time in the swimming pool, or running up and down the beach. We were introduced to Wonder Bread and sliced process cheese, and these became our staples for those two weeks in the motel.

My grandmother was our baby sitter while my parents went out to look for a car. We were going to drive across the United States, and needed something large enough for us to make the journey. It turned out to be a shiny, brand new, pale green 1960 Buick Le Sabre two-door hardtop with air-conditioning. The trunk was huge, but barely large enough to accommodate all our suitcases. Loading and arranging all the stuff was quite the process, with no space wasted—it was packed to the rafters. That car, laden with so much humanity and baggage, sat low to the ground, an ocean freighter full of cargo. We were low riders!

We worked out a seating arrangement that today would be illegal. Dad drove; mom and grandmother took turns sitting in the front passenger seat, and one of us kids sat between them. In the back seat four of us squished in, with the two-year old on someone's lap.

Dad insisted the only way the air-conditioning would work was if all the windows were closed. Unfortunately, my dad and grand-mother were chain smokers, and my mom an occasional one. So there we were, held captive for hours at a time in a cramped space full of second-hand smoke. Any time we pulled into a gas station or stopped to eat, we kids would fall out of the car looking green and gasping for fresh air.

Dad was not proud of having subjected us to so much second-hand smoke. Fortunately, he quit smoking cold turkey in 1963 on the day he learned one of his older brothers, who had smoked most of his adult life, had died from emphysema.

I was sad to leave the coast as we travelled north through cen-tral Florida. This had been my first time seeing and experiencing the ocean, and I would have liked to stay close to the coast. Further north, we had a cousin who lived in South Carolina and, before heading west, we drove up to see him and to meet his wife. The thing I re-member most about that leg of the journey were the amazing apple pies his wife baked from scratch when we arrived. They were deep and delicious. How much more American could you get?

As we made our way west through Alabama and Mississippi, we were always on the lookout for Howard Johnson's restaurants. My older sister, Carmen, was in love with, if not addicted to, their strawberry milk shakes, and we were all in love with their cheese-burgers. I was learning new phrases, "Cheese burger, please," and "Thank you very much." My English was non-existent, but thanks to Carmen, I was kept somewhat informed as to what was being said and what was going on.

You can imagine what goes through the mind of a ten-year-old who has lost all sense of proportion and relevance. I'm sure my younger sister Angela, who was five at the time, felt just as discombobulated as I did. John, the two year-old, would have been oblivious to everything, while my older brother, Enrique, almost fourteen, and Carmen, the oldest at 16, would have had a better grasp of our new adventure. I was full of questions and very unsure about how I was supposed to act. I resorted to what had worked for me in Colombia: I studied Enrique and did as he did. I liked what he liked, hated what he hated, and spoke like he spoke.

I was a bed wetter. Not a small problem to have on a trip like this. I wonder how many motel mattresses I ruined? It didn't help my self-esteem either, which always seemed to be running on empty. What I mean by this is, when you think about it, self-esteem is the result of how we view ourselves in comparison to others. When we conclude we are inferior in one way or another, and if this inferior quality appears to be out of one's control or won't go away despite our best efforts, then bingo, we have low self-esteem. It is as if I was born with a set of balance scales in hand. I was always weighing things, making comparisons, looking for similarities and differences. And bedwetting was certainly a difference. No one else in my family wet their bed. Why was I the only one?

Chapter 2: California, Here We Come

The fall of 1960 was a pivotal time for my family. For me, it was also when I came face to face with my vulnerabilities, compounded by the fact I could not speak the language. Arriving in a new country does not have to be traumatic, and for the most part my experience was anything but. But I remember moments of sheer panic, some of which in retrospect, are funny to me now.

For example: when we visited the subterranean caves in Carlsbad, New Mexico en route to California, we were three thousand feet below the surface, and I needed to go to the restroom. Dad pointed me in the direction of the facilities, and off I went. I spotted a sign that ended with "MEN"—that much I recognized—and entered. I found myself smack in the middle of the ladies' washroom, with all of them staring at me like an interloper. After what seemed like an eternity of stunned silence I dashed back out of there, but stopped to examine the sign one more time. "WOMEN," I concluded, must mean the other sex. Across the passageway I saw another sign that only said "MEN" and entered cautiously.

Yes, it's a cute story, but at times like these I had just wanted the earth to open up and swallow me whole. I have always overthought things and have had a hyper sensitive, well-developed sense of guilt and shame—that's the only way I can describe it. I'm the person who sees a cop and automatically sticks his hands out to be handcuffed. I am convinced peer pressure was less oppressive than the judgments I passed on myself for things I was not responsible for. I was pretty hard on myself. If I did succeed in something, whatever success and praise I might enjoy was soon overshadowed by the sense of inadequacy and insecurity that always dogged me.

During this trek across the Southern states, I stayed close to Enrique. This was especially true when we went to Disneyland in California. He was charged with keeping an eye on me, which meant we took the same rides, including the Matterhorn. That was great. I always felt secure when I was with him; he was my protector. I know later on, such as when I was a freshman in high school and he a junior, this taking care of little brother became something he despised. "Yes, you can borrow the car to go to the basketball game, but take your brother with you," my mom would say. Those words were a bitter pill to him, and at times he resented me.

I recognized at an early age that, though I tried to be just like Enrique, there were things he did or said, or things he liked, that just did not seem to fit me. Too introspective and insecure to realize it was natural to feel this way, I forced myself to try harder to be like him. Without realizing it, I was developing the skill that served me well all my life: the suppression of who I really am.

In the larger scheme of things, there was nothing extraordinary about the uprooting and transplanting of our family. No generation, tribe or nationality has been immune to a yearning to live in a different land, in a better place, regardless of the cost. If there was a price to be paid for our relocation, it was paid in large part by my grandmother and my mom. They lost their social and family standings, and were cut off from everything that defined them. By comparison, we kids were a bit more resilient and more adaptable; consequently our sense of isolation and detachment was short-lived, but it was not so for them.

Dad was the visionary and the driving force behind this adventure and, though he severed his business ties with his brothers, moving to the U.S. was something he had wanted to do since the day he got married. At the age of eighteen, he left Colombia on a steamship and arrived in New York City with twenty dollars in his pocket. Unlike his two older brothers, who had been educated in the United States and were both civil engineers, my grandfather had refused to pay for my dad's education as punishment for not having been a straight "A" student like his brothers had been. He decided to do it on his own, and did not leave on good terms with his father.

In New York, he slept at the YMCA when he could afford it and, since he could not speak English, learned to survive doing all kinds of low-paying jobs. Little by little he was able to pull himself up by his bootstraps, eventually becoming secretary to an executive in Dayton, Ohio. He learned to type, to write in shorthand, and to do general office work. Then he received a telegram from one of his brothers with the news their father was dying, imploring him to come home to make peace with him. He returned to Colombia a few months before the Japanese attacked Pearl Harbor in December 1941. In mid November he met my mom at one of his older brother's birthday party. For now, there would be no going to the U.S. He had always intended to return to the U.S. as soon as possible, but that would have to wait now that there was a war on and he was in love.

How and why we ended up in San Jose, California, has everything to do with my parent's friendship with the Sisters of Marymount. This was a Roman Catholic religious order from New York, which ran a handful of all-girl schools in the U.S. They also had a school in Bogotá, where Carmen had been enrolled, so my parents decided to live in America where the sisters had one of their schools. Since mom did not relish the idea of living anywhere snow fell, and most of the schools were on the East Coast with cold snowy winters, these were quickly ruled out. The choice was then between their two schools in California. One was in Palos Verdes near Long Beach, and the other was in San Jose, south of San Francisco.

I'm not entirely sure why San Jose won out, but I think it was its proximity to the much beloved San Francisco, and the fact the weather was a bit milder than that of Los Angeles. Extreme heat and snow were to be avoided.

We arrived in San Jose on US 101, and pulled into a motel on that busy highway. It was a far cry from the motel in Miami, which had been resort-like. Since the plan was for my parents to find a house for us, we would be staying at this motel until the deed was done. For two weeks we endured this boring little corner of San Jose. The motel coincidentally was downwind of an Ac'cent plant, so we got to breath copious amounts of MSG-laden stinky air. It got in your throat and left a horrible taste in your mouth.

The tourist part of our adventure had come to an end, and now we were in a kind of limbo state. We did nothing but watch TV from the moment we awoke until we went to sleep at night. Call it Cultural Immersion 101. You name it, we watched it: *The Price is Right, Captain Kangaroo, Andy Griffith, Route 66, My Three Sons, Surfside 6*—and of course *I Love Lucy*—just to name a few.

Repetition is always good when one is trying to learn a new language, so the repetitious nature of daytime television was welcome, and provided us with several new phrases and words. In and of themselves, these would have been meaningless, but were made comprehensible when attached to moving images and facial expressions.

The house my parents purchased was in one of the many brand new subdivisions that were starting to consume the picturesque, orchard-laden Santa Clara Valley. At the time there was this social divide between the East and West Valley. The Mexican, Chicanos and blacks lived in East San Jose. It was also the older half of the city, and was not enjoying the rapid development of West San Jose.

Our subdivision was called Primrose Lane. Phase I was almost sold out and Phase II was under construction. The sound of hammers and electric saws was constant for almost a year after we moved in. Many of the new owners were aerospace workers at massive facilities for companies like Lockheed and General Electric; Silicon Valley was not yet a reality.

Families with two or more kids were the rule rather than the exception, so we fit right in—sort of. Most of these newly occupied houses sat on barren adobe-like dirt lots with no landscaping. That is how the houses were sold: it was up to the homeowners to seed their lawns, plant their trees and shrubs, and do their own landscaping. Not ours: my parents managed to buy one of the four display homes on Camellia Way, which boasted a designer yard, fully landscaped. We did not have to lift a finger; we had the complete turn-key package.

With the purchase of the house complete, the next task at hand for my parents was to acquire all the furnishings and household items we would need. We took possession of the house and for the first few days, we "made do" as delivery trucks arrived with mattresses, bureaus, chairs, tables, sofas and linen. Curiosity drew kids from up and down the block whenever a truck pulled up, and, little by little, we began to recognize our neighbors, with whom we exchanged friendly gestures since we were unable to communicate any other way.

Chapter 3: Growing Roots

As new routines were slowly being established in our new home, they marked the end of this amazing trip we had been on. I finally surrendered to the scary reality of going to school in a foreign country. Angela and I were placed in a public elementary school, she in kindergarten, and me in fifth grade. Enrique went to a public junior high school for seventh grade, and Carmen was enrolled as a junior at Mother Butler Memorial High School, the Marymount school. We kids attended three different schools: Carmen had to be driven to and from hers each day, but the rest of us were picked up by yellow school buses and taken to our respective destinations.

There were two fifth grade classes at Moreland Elementary School. I was placed in Mr. Bennett's class. The principal, Mrs. Anderson, a grandmotherly woman, thought this was the best choice for me, since Mr. Bennett spoke Spanish. As I mentioned earlier, Hispanics lived in the East Side and, as a result, I was a bit of a novelty at this school. I don't remember any other foreign nationals there who were, in today's parlance, English as Second Language (ESL).

Mr. Bennett reminded me of Perry Mason. He had presence when he stood in the front of the class, just as when Perry Mason stood in front of the court. I was introduced to the class the first day, and was given a seat at the back of the classroom next to the arts and crafts tables. That first morning during the first recess, my curious classmates asked me many questions, but I didn't understand them.

In the first week one boy in particular took me under his wing. He was a big kid, a freckle-faced strawberry blonde boy whose dad was a captain in the fire department. His name was John, and I remember him because he gently pulled me aside one day, using gestures and speaking slowly to explained how running in the hallways was forbidden by the school principal, and how I would get into trouble if I continued to do it. Gratefully, I thought to myself, "Oh boy, I sure don't want to get in trouble."

There were several other rules I soon became aware of, such as the invisible line that separated the playground between the first to fourth graders from the fifth and sixth graders. I found this out the hard way when I ventured into the wrong side, and was soon surrounded by a mob of fourth grade boys who took delight in taunting me. Some of them pushed and poked me, while others yelled stuff that was completely unintelligible to me. I did recognize one phrase, "Stupid Mexican!" Fortunately, my new big friend John came to my rescue, pulling me to safety beyond the invisible line.

Before we knew it, a month had gone by since we arrived from Colombia. My tenth birthday was approaching, and life was beginning to fall into place for us kids. This birthday would be the first of our birthdays to be celebrated with only our immediate family and not the whole extended family of aunts, uncles, and our many cousins, as had been the custom for us in Colombia. From now on, things were going to be very different.

When the trunks with our belongings finally arrived in San Francisco and were brought to the house, mom and my grandmother busied themselves unpacking silverware, clothing and you-name-it. They made the house feel like home, adding their little touches here and there, though the smell of naphthalene mothballs permeated the house for days.

Dad was now busy thinking about how he would support the family, since the money my parents and grandmother had saved for this adventure was slowly being depleted. The only cash flow the family had was the rent money from the house in Bogotá. Fortunately, the rent was paid in U.S. dollars. The exchange rate for the Colombian *peso* was seven-to-one on the day we left. I know this for a fact, because my dad exchanged my cigar box containing seven *pesos* worth of Colombian coins for one American dollar. I say fortunately for us the rent money was in dollars, because the exchange rate continued to deteriorate each passing day. If the rent had been paid in *pesos*, it would have spelled disaster.

Dad chose to enroll in night school to study for his California real estate license. After all, San Jose was a boomtown and houses were being built at breakneck speed. What better industry to focus on? Encouraged by his conversations with the agents who worked at Primrose Lane, he approached Stone and Schulte Realty, whose signs seemed to be everywhere. Once dad had his license, he was assigned to an office in East San Jose that served the Chicano and Mexican community. This seemed like the perfect fit for my dad. Since he spoke Spanish, he was soon fielding leads left and right. However, success became elusive. For every five offers he processed that were subject to finance, only one would qualify. Eighty percent of his time was being eaten up by these failed sales. His take-home pay was disproportionate to the amount of work he was doing when compared to his English language-only counterparts.

The romance of life in America was beginning to lose some of its luster and magic for my mom, who had enjoyed having maids in Colombia who did the cooking, house cleaning and laundry. Now she was doing it all. My grandmother was no slouch either. She pitched in and watched over us whenever my parents went out. I remember looking at her with admiration, and sensing that she was lonely. We were the only social contact she had; yet she was always lovingly positive and reassuring. Because she spoke no English her isolation was complete. Her contact with the outside world was a *Realistic* transistor radio with a shortwave band. She listened to Spanish broadcasts follow her favored *novellas (soaps)*. Aside from that, even watching TV with us was not as enjoyable for her, except for variety shows such as *Lawrence Welk* and the *Ed Sullivan Show*.

However, this is what she wanted for us. Mom was reluctant to leave Colombia, but my grandmother told her she should think about the future of her children in Colombia, especially in view of the events in Cuba. She added that she was willing to give up everything for her grandchildren so they could have this opportunity of a lifetime. For my parents, that helped to tip the scale in favor of coming to the U.S. They had agonized about how our move would affect my grandmother; mom was an only child, and leaving her mother alone in Colombia was not an option.

Wanting so badly to fit in motivated us to learn English. In those days there were no ESL classes, it was sink or swim for Enrique, my younger sister Angela, and me. Carmen had a good command of English, thanks to her many years in school with the American Sisters in Bogotá. In class, Mr. Bennett allowed me to take part in math and science, since, as it turned out, in forth grade I had already studied what was being taught in fifth grade in California. Mr. Bennet also included me in the vocabulary and spelling quizzes he gave every week.

The rest of the time he had me sit at one of the art tables in the back of the classroom with a stack of old Sears catalogs and magazines, a pair of scissors, a bottle of glue and large newsprint scrapbooks. My assignment was to cut out objects, paste them into the book, and write down their names: toaster, tire, dress, hat, pants, glove, rake, vacuum cleaner, etc. I got to draw pictures of objects too. Since I am artistic, I had lots of fun at the back of the class.

My classmates were always surprised at how well I did in the spelling tests. My secret was that I was learning the words phonetically and pronounced them as if they were Spanish words. When Mr. Bennett would call out the words, I would sound them out in my head in Spanish, and that was it—it worked almost one hundred percent of the time. The vocabulary tests were usually multiple-choice, but I gradually began to understand and pick out the correct definitions.

Chapter 4: A New Awareness

Fifth grade for me was definitely a year full of new experiences. Among them was being in a coed class for the first time. The schools I attended in Colombia separated the boys from the girls. For boys and girls my last school even had different bus schedules, start times, and lunch periods. We never saw each other; for each it was as if the other sex didn't exist. Now I was realizing things about myself that were very confusing, and I didn't know how to make sense of these conflicting feelings, thoughts, and questions.

This conundrum in my head was all the more overwhelming when combined with all the other issues that were part of being new in a foreign country and not knowing the language. Insecure and introspective, I never said anything to anyone, not just out of embarrassment, but because I wasn't able to explain myself in a way that would make sense. It was as if there was yet another language I still had to learn.

These were not new feelings or questions. I had felt them for as long as I could remember, and however confusing and puzzling they were, I had no words to describe them. My new proximity to girls was both fascinating and scary. Though I had many female first cousins and had been around them whenever our extended family celebrated all manner of occasions, there was really very little interaction between the boys and the girls. Boys were put together to play with boys, and girls with girls. I was far enough in age from both of my sisters that, even at home, there was not that much interaction between us. With the move to the States I was suddenly exposed to girls my age on a daily basis, and, put simply, I was unprepared.

There was one little girl in my class whose name was Marsha. I don't know why I found myself transfixed by her. The dress code was still very conservative in those days, and girls wore skirts or dresses that went down to their knees. You never saw a girl in pants or shorts unless they were worn under their skirts for going out in the playground. Marsha loved swinging and hanging from the monkey bars, and she always wore a pair of capris under her skirt. This allowed her to hang upside down from the bars and to swing herself without fear of her skirt going up over her face.

I think that was the first time I experienced an awareness that I wished I were a girl. This thought was quickly doused with a bucketfull of self-recrimination and self-ridicule. How could I be so silly? And what if anyone found out I had this crazy notion in my head?

Marsha's dad was either laid off or transferred, and her family moved away halfway through the school year. Their house was a few blocks away from ours and, the weekend after their departure, I went to the empty duplex where they had lived and looked in through the windows. Why, I would ask myself, was I not a girl like she was, since I felt more comfortable with that idea than I did with the idea of being a boy?

This was the million-dollar question. And it was also the beginning of trying to make sense of this feeling of disconnection I had with my body. From my earliest memories I knew that something was not quite right with my body.

For example, I don't know how old I was at the time, but it is a "moving picture" as sharp in my memory today as if it happened yesterday. I was sitting in the bathtub playing with a couple of toys. I happened to get a glance of myself, my genitals, and I instinctively grabbed the washcloth placed on the edge of the bathtub and covered myself with it. I wanted to hide that part of my body because it made me uncomfortable seeing it. This little behavior was often repeated.

Then, a little older now, standing in the shower, I never allowed myself to look down to that region of my body. If I dropped the soap,

I would squat down and feel for it rather than run the risk of seeing myself. Alternatively, I would find the soap with my feet, close my eyes, and bend down to pick it up. Such were the kind of tactics I resorted to avoid seeing my genitals.

Often parents of transgender individuals are asked if they perceived or noticed anything different about their child that might have hinted at something being wrong or different. And often the answer is that there were no indications of anything amiss, that they didn't see any red flags. There could be several explanations for this; one is the parents were not very attentive; another, the parents were attentive but not very bright; yet another, they may have noticed something, but considered it a harmless phase of growing up, a natural curiosity not requiring intervention. I think the latter is closest to what happened to me. My parents were lovingly unassuming and confident all was okay. There was also the fact that I did everything possible to hide my "oddity," and learned to deflect attention by acting according to their expectations.

From accounts of transgender individuals I have met, one learns stealth and deception at an early age—not out of malice, but as a way to survive. For me, as the pressure and the need to act normal increased, I always worried about being found out. What if I said something in my sleep, or what if I accidentally let some embarrassing secret slip out in a conversation? It is not that I was engaging in all kinds of secret and odd behavior; I wasn't. It was all the stuff in my head that never seemed to get resolved.

There was one incident, however. For our first summer in California, my parents surprised us with the addition of an above ground swimming pool. A neighbor had installed one in a day—it was an instant swimming pool! What a great idea, especially since summers in San Jose were much hotter than anything we were used to.

One afternoon, everyone seemed to be off doing something: my grandmother was in her room as always, my siblings were with friends, dad was at work—and my mom, well, I was soon to find out, was also at home. I was alone in the backyard near the swimming pool, mesmerized as I watched trails of tiny black ants make their way across the hot cement patio. As I played with them by putting obstacles in their way, I spotted Carmen's one-piece swimsuit hanging on one of the rungs of the pool ladder. I went up to it and touched it, as if to see if it would bite. Suddenly I had this crazy idea to put it on. I grabbed it and stepped behind some waist-high shrubs under my parent's bedroom window, quickly stripped off my clothes, and slipped into the suit. It was way too big on me and hung down unceremoniously.

No sooner had I put it on than I heard a loud knocking on the window above me. It was my mom, shaking her head and signaling "No! No!" with her index finger. I don't think Superman ever changed as fast as I did in that moment. I re-hung the suit on the ladder and was expecting my mom to come out to yell at me. But she didn't. That anticipation was probably worse, and I agonized like crazy. After a while, thinking my life was over and completely overcome with embarrassment, I sneaked back into the house and into my room to wait for the world to end. Dad was going to be home soon, and I figured mom was going to delegate justice to him as she had done many times in the past.

But nothing happened. Mom just shrugged it off as normal boy's curiosity. That was my first experience with wearing a girl's piece of clothing, and the guilt, shame, and embarrassment I felt went off the charts.

By the time sixth grade began in the fall of 1961 we had been in the U.S. just under a year. My new teacher, Mrs. Lewin, lived directly across the street from us. Though my English was much better by then, I still misunderstood things. A couple of weeks before school started in September there was a neighborhood get-together one evening, and Mrs. Lewin pulled me aside to tell me she was going to be my new teacher. I wasn't exactly sure I understood everything she said to me, and when she saw the puzzled look on my face she asked if I was unhappy about being in her class. I understood the word "happy" in her question and answered "Yes!" With a worried look on her face, she asked me one more time, and I gave her the same answer. Finally she asked with a sad look on her face, "You don't want to be in my class?" I finally understood what she was asking me, and I answered, "Yes, I want to be in your class." Then it dawned on me that "unhappy" was the opposite of "happy." Darn those compound English words!

The school where I attended sixth and seventh grades was the brand-new Rogers Junior High School. Opened just that year, it didn't offer eighth grade until the second year, when the seventh graders moved up. It was quite different being in a brand new classroom. This was a first for me. All the schools I attended in Colombia had been around for years. Even Moreland Elementary was also an old school, built before the Second World War. To me, old schools always had a smell that was a combination of floor wax and old plywood desks, combined with a rubbery sort of aroma. On hot days at Moreland this smell was really pronounced. But at Rogers everything smelled new.

I don't have too many memories of sixth grade, other than I only knew fewer than half the students in the class, since the new junior high drew students from several elementary schools. Nonetheless, I was getting to know people, and life was somehow working itself out. Inwardly, my insecurities were ever present, but still a mixture with those related to my being in a new country. My preoccupation with my body and the intense desire to assimilate and be like everyone else were at the core of my doubts and feelings of inferiority. I could not shed the feeling something was not right with me. I could not understand it.

In many ways I believe that, when faced with the unknown, we

yearn for things to be black and white, to be this or that; we want—
we need—clarity. If, for whatever reason, we are unsure of things,
and things don't fall neatly into what we can understand, it can be
paralyzing and frightening. My narrow view of the world and my linear way of thinking caused me much anguish.

Of course I was a boy, I would argue with myself; I had the body
of a boy. Bear in mind, for the first eleven years of my life I didn't really know what the biological differences were between boys and
girls. I was only aware of the superficial differences, such as girls had
long hair, boys had short hair; girls wore frilly soft colored skirts and
dresses and ribbons in their hair, while boys wore pants and dark col-
ors; girls played with dolls, and boys with guns and toy trucks. That
was my understanding of the gender differences. That is not to say I
was attracted to the girly things, as one might expect me to have been.
My likes and wants were carbon copies of those of my brother
Enrique.

I'm not sure I can really explain this to your—or to my—satisfaction. I may begin to sound like a broken record, but I beat myself
up for not knowing how I should act, and the path of least resistance
seemed to be to mimic my brother. He obviously did not have this
anxiety about what he was, and I envied him for that. Ironically, I
also grew to be repulsed at his level of comfort with his own body.
How could he not be turned off with his body in the same way I was
with mine? With time, I could see the changes in his body that were
taking place. After all, he was well into puberty, and whiskers and
body hair were beginning to appear on him. I was horrified for my
brother.

In Colombia, we had belonged to one of Bogotá's exclusive golf
and country clubs, known as "Los Lagartos" (The Lizards). My parents were charter members and, since the founding of the golf course,
they had both learned the game well. We spent many weekends at
the club. It was an amazing place. It had its own lagoon large enough

for ski boats, two swimming pools, tennis courts, and acres and acres of undeveloped property within its gates. It was a playground beyond comparison.

On occasion, I would have to go with my dad into the clubhouse and men's locker room. There I often saw men who were only covered with a towel around their waist I don't really remember seeing anything else. I assumed women and girls probably did the same thing, but I really did not know how else they might be different. The only other impression I recall was the amount of body hair on some of those men; for some reason I found that very troubling.

Now that I think about it, there was a boy my age I often saw running around with his friends. The reasons he stands out in my mind is because one day he fell into one of the swimming pools with his clothes on. His mother rushed him into the women's changing room to change out of his wet clothes. When they emerged, the boy was wearing a girl's swimming suit. He resumed play, not the least worried about what anybody thought.

That incident in itself did not take on any significance for me—until the day I accidentally fell into the lagoon with my clothes on. I was about five years old when this happened. I thought about the boy as I was being taken back dripping to my parents, and the thought crossed my mind that I, too, was going to change out of my clothes and into a girl's swimming suit.

No such luck. I was just wrapped in towels while my damp clothes were wrung out and then put back on me. Why, I wondered, did they not treat me as the other boy's parents had treated him? Somehow I felt deprived.

The story I shared with you earlier about when my mom found me trying on my sister's swimming suit was a long time after this incident, but I couldn't help but feel the same way—deprived or denied—except in my San Jose experience I also felt ashamed.

Chapter 5: How American

Back on the family front, the first two years in California in terms of adjustments were probably the most intense. The tract home we lived in was barely large enough to house a family of eight. My mom and grandmother, bless their souls, had to recalibrate their recipes about cooking times. At the elevation of Bogotá—more than 8,300 feet above sea level—it takes twice as long to boil water. Consequently, there were many burnt meals in San Jose at first.

Most of our meals in Colombia would have been cooked from scratch, and such things as leafy greens, though available in the market, were only used as garnish and seldom consumed, as they were too commonly contaminated with salmonella and other nasty things. We ate plenty of rice, kidney beans, and potatoes, along with some kind of protein. Our meat was always well done and our vegetables boiled to death.

Compared to the bounty of food and all the possibilities that were available in San Jose's supermarkets, our diet in Colombia didn't vary too much. The novel discovery for us in California was the frozen TV dinner and other packaged meals. These solved several problems, since mom was tired of running a "hotel." Now we could pick the entree of our choosing. It was such a modern way to do things but I don't think there was a single family member who didn't put on additional pounds, and they came on quickly. Our bodies just soaked up all those calories.

So by the time seventh grade approached in the fall of 1962, I now had another problem—I was chubby and much more self-conscious than I had ever been. I was horrified to learn that, from seventh grade on up, one had to shower at the end of P.E. class. Physical education was a daily thing, and there was no getting around it.

I was almost nauseous the first day we changed into our P.E. clothes, and then showered at the end of the period. I did not want to face anyone when we came into the locker room to shower. I made my way from my locker to the closest six-headed shower pole with one arm folded against my jiggling chest and the other holding up the towel I had wrapped around my waist, just like I had seen the men in the country club do. It wasn't long before those in my stall started laughing at me. Then, to my horror, someone yanked the towel out of my hand. Someone else said, "Look at the tiny dick!" More laughter.

If ever there was a moment when I wanted to just vanish into thin air, this was it.

Not a good way to start the school year. From that day on, until my 21st birthday, when California law exempted one from P.E. classes (even in college and university), I had to grin and bare it—pardon the pun. I am not kidding, my heart was always in my throat and, to deal with it, I determined to always run to the locker room to be one of the first in and out of the showers and into my clothes. If for some reason I was delayed, I would then wait for as many to shower before I would venture in. Naturally, I never could talk to anyone about my little hang-up.

Post-traumatic stress is now recognized as a serious medical condition, and there are support systems available to those who may be suffering from it. This wasn't necessarily the case in the early sixties. Would things be different for me if someone could have intervened? I'm not sure. Much of my confusion predated a couple of events in my life, which alone would qualify me for therapy today.

The first took place in the fall of 1962. Like Enrique, I, too, had started to deliver newspapers. His route was predominantly in our subdivision, whereas mine was across Williams Road, the main artery that fed our streets. On the south side of Williams Road there were several blocks of two-story apartment buildings. I delivered the afternoon San Jose News to about eighty apartments.

At the end of every month, I would go door-to-door to collect three dollars from each customer. It often took several tries before I would find any given customer at home. One night as I began my rounds, I knocked on one door, but there was no answer. I started down the stairs when I heard the door open behind me. A man called out, "Who's there?"

I said I was the paperboy collecting for the paper. He asked me to come back up. When I got to the door I saw he was wrapped in a towel. He apologized and said he was just about to step into the shower. He invited me in and closed the door while he went to the bedroom to get his wallet.

Through all of this, I kept thinking it was okay to see a man seminude, and not to worry since he was covered in a towel—simply take the cash, I thought, give him his receipt, and get out of there. Imagine my shock when he returned to the living room without the towel, and sporting a raging erection. I didn't know where to look except down at the receipt book in my hands. He handed me the money, but as I went to take it, he grabbed my hand and pulled me into the bedroom warning me to stay quiet. There he proceeded to masturbate with my hand wrapped around his penis. What resistance I offered was no match for his strength, and I could not pull away. I could not bear to look at what he was doing, and just wished I had never been born. After he ejaculated and wiped his and my hand with a towel, he threatened me to not tell anyone. I left his apartment quickly, and don't remember anything else about that night, except washing my hands with soap for a very long time.

I was afraid of telling my parents, of telling Enrique. I never did. Not only was I terrified of this man, I was afraid that if I said anything about what he had done to me my parents would take us all back to Colombia. And if the police were called, I feared, we would be deported: how shameful that would be if I ruined everything for the rest of my family! On top of it all, I felt like I was the guilty one, and that what had happened was my all fault.

The second incident took place when I was fifteen. But before I share that experience, I need to fill you in on what transpired between 1961 and 1965. Of course there were other events that affected us as a family which had an impact on the decision my parents would make. I don't need to elaborate on the Cuban missile crisis, except to say that we all breathed a sigh of relief to be in the U.S. then since there was fear about what may happen to Colombia if the Cuban-inspired Communist guerrillas succeeded. I remember the air raid drills, the low flying military jets, and all the hysteria of those few weeks when things got a little intense.

By the summer of 1963, my parents had decided we needed a bigger house. There was a new subdivision being built and this time they could customize aspects and features of a six bedroom, two-story house, which was in the construction stage. It meant Angela and I had to change schools; Enrique would continue attending the same high school. Carmen was now enrolled at Foothill College in Los Altos.

Earlier I pointed out our house in Bogotá was leased for three years, as the plan was that we might return to Colombia. There was a lot of intense discussion about this, and Enrique was quite outspoken about how terrible it would be for him to return to Bogotá, as he would then lose a school year. He had done the math and, because of his birth month and the different school year calendars, he would have to repeat the year he had just completed. Plus, he argued, if they had given Carmen the opportunity to graduate from the Marymount nun's school, then he, too, should be allowed to finish high school in California. Of course there were other reasons for it, but my parents finally made the decision to sell the house in Colombia.

Unfortunately, real estate prices are not pegged to the value of the local currency's exchange rate. This meant that though the house in Bogotá had appreciated in value, the increase was nowhere near the new exchange rate. When the Colombian currency from the sale of the house was converted to U.S. dollars, my parents found that they had lost a lot of their personal worth. Whatever money they received went into the new house. The sale of the Camellia Way house in San Jose, on the market for a long time, did not result in any great capital gain, as layoffs at Lockheed had resulted in a surplus of housing. It was a buyer's market.

We moved into the new house at about the same time school started in the fall of 1963. It was so much better for living space. But I was upset to leave Rogers Junior High and all my friends behind. If it is stressful for regular kids to be a new kid in school, it was doubly hard for me. Just when I was starting to feel comfortable with one group of people I would have to start over with a new group. I didn't like being an outsider, and that is exactly how I felt.

I complained to Enrique that I didn't want to go to a different school, but he pointed out that I would get to be with my old friends again in ninth grade when I started at Blackford High School. He thought I was lucky since I would know twice as many people as those who had only attended one junior high school. He would have liked that for himself. He helped me see it in an entirely different light.

Chapter 6: A Sticky Situation

Always the introvert, I was also the epitome of a prude, so oblivious and ignorant to and of so many things. The new neighborhood had many larger homes with large families like ours. Across the street lived a family with about four kids. The second youngest was a year younger than me, and we became friends. He was a little fatter than me and he reminded me a bit of Beaver's chubby friend Gus in *Leave it to Beaver*. We were playing one day when he asked me if I wanted to jack off with him. I didn't know what he was talking about. I shook my head because I didn't understand the question, which he interpreted as a "no." He was suddenly very defensive, and reassured me it was okay because his older brothers did it all the time. I still didn't know what he was talking about. I sensed he was upset with me for not wanting to join him, but I didn't know what he meant by "jacking off." I don't remember playing with him after that, and he never came over again.

By now I had a better understanding of the differences between girls and boys, but I still did not have a clue about the facts of life. My chubbiness was a huge source of embarrassment for me, since it resulted in my having little pointy breasts. Though I now also wished I was a girl, I was also painfully aware that I wasn't. Yet my body did not look like other boys' bodies, either. They were flat chested and fit, I was soft and plump, and to top it all, I was a late bloomer. I was okay with it in one sense because it meant I still did not have any body hair.

There was another difference between the two junior high schools I attended. Because the junior high school I transferred to was old, it didn't have showers in the locker room. You can't imagine how ecstatic I was when I discovered this. We still had to change in and out of our P.E. clothes, but I didn't have to endure the indignity of walking twenty feet without any clothes on. This horror would be postponed for one year, when I would start ninth grade at Blackford High School.

It was during this last year in junior high school that JFK was assassinated, and the Beatles arrived from England. The first two events were very sad, but I'll never forget the frenzied excitement all the girls had over the Beatles. I, too, got swept up like everyone. I was just learning to play guitar, and it wasn't long before Beatles song-books were available, showing guitar chords of the Beatles' songs. I was hooked. I wasn't very good, but eventually learned to strum the guitar, and spent many hours playing Beatles songs in my room, and later with friends.

The paper route I had when we lived on Camellia Way had been turned over to a different boy, since we were now too far from the old neighborhood for me to continue. I was able to get a route near the new house. However, instead of delivering the afternoon edition of the *San Jose News,* as I had in the previous route, I now delivered the morning edition of the *San Jose Mercury-News.* This meant I had to get up by 5:30 A.M. so I could be done in time to get ready for school.

I was well into this daily routine, being really quiet when I got up so as not to wake anybody. I would exit through the garage where the bikes were kept, and to get to it I had to pass through the laundry room. One morning, as I walked past the washer and dryer, I notice a neatly folded stack of my sister's clothing. On top were several pairs of nylon underwear. I had the same reaction I had with that one-piece swimsuit, and was overcome with curiosity. Knowing no one else was up, I decided to put them on to see if they fit. They did. Suddenly a pang of guilt ran through me, and I took them off and refolded them as I had found them before getting out of there as quickly as I could.

Seeing stacks of clothing like that did not happen very often, but now I was aware of their presence whenever they were there. I repeated this a few more times with the same kind of reaction, but in the process I became aware of how I felt somehow more comfortable with myself with them on than I did wearing my own boy's undershorts.

One morning I finally decided to wear them under my clothes when I went out to deliver the papers. However, when I got home I had a problem to solve. In my blinded indulgence I had not realized the pair I wore was the only pair on that particular stack of folded laundry. Someone was going to notice them missing.

I had planned to simply take them off and place them with a pile of dirty clothes that were in the hamper, hoping that no one would be the wiser. People would be starting to get up soon and I had to think quickly. Simply folding them and putting them back after having worn them for almost and hour and a half was not going to work. What to do? My solution was to take them to the bathroom and rinse them with some hand soap, towel dry them the best I could, and then placed them over the heater vent in the floor of the bathroom. Fortunately the furnace was blowing warm air, and the damp nylon fabric dried quickly. That morning I bit the bullet.

This curiosity of mine, I must emphasize, was not sexualized. It was not a source of stimulation, and neither was it in any way a sexual fetish. As I mentioned, I was a late bloomer and had not yet started puberty; therefore, I was not aroused when I wore these items. I simply felt at peace and calm in a way that transcended the sense of disconnection I felt with my body.

In my mind, I really had a major dilemma. I knew I was risking getting caught, and the thought of doing so horrified me. I also knew if I ever told anyone of what I was doing I would become a laughing stock, ostracized and labeled forever. I would have to be more careful and secretive than I had ever been in my life.

The differences between my friends and me had also become more acute. Whenever my friends talked about girls now they would say stuff that was either over my head or insulting. And because I, too, felt insulted, I identified more with the girls than I did with my friends. This was also a cause for the need to be careful and secretive. I had to be careful not to act in a way that was different from them, or to say anything that might reveal my true thoughts. I did not want to be rejected by them.

These differences were also somewhat noticeable with my older brother, Enrique. In the new house I no longer shared a bedroom with him, so, as we seldom spent time together any more, I was less conscious of our differences.

How else was I naïve? One night in Catechism class (which, as a Catholic, I attended once a week at our parish church), we were given a piece of paper, and asked to write down what we knew of the facts of life, and to then fold the paper in half and place it on the teacher's desk at the front of the class. We were assured no one except the couple who were our teachers would get to see these. I didn't know what they were asking, and raised my hand for clarification. I had no idea why my question was met with so much snickering from my classmates. The woman teacher came up to me as said, "Tell us what you know about the birds and the bees."

"Oh!" I exclaimed, "The birds and the bees!" I still had no clue why they were asking such a question, so I wrote about birds and bees, that they both had wings and flew. This couple must have laughed their guts out that night when they read my answer. I'm still embarrassed thinking about it.

How can anyone be so ignorant about sex at the age of thirteen? Lucky me, I was. There had been times when I had asked my dad specific questions, such as on the day he picked me up from school in Bogotá, and told me I had a baby brother. I was so surprised.

"Where did he come from?" I asked. I was almost eight years

old at the time, and the answer he gave me satisfied my need to know.

"He was with the angels," my dad said, "and God sent him down to us." I had not even known my mom was pregnant—but my not knowing that was by design. In those days, pregnant women were camouflaged somehow, and their pregnancy was not on public display. Sex was never discussed at home; kids learned these things on the playground. Perhaps the language barrier contributed to my missing out on the intelligence. I just never got the message.

Chapter 7: On the Meaning of Words

Would things be different for me now had I learned these things sooner? Before you jump to a positive conclusion and determine this is a perfect example of why sex education is so important, remember that I was already aware that I was somehow different well before I could have understood sexuality. A good dose of sex education would not have helped this inner sense of conflict about my identity. It probably would have provided me with more distress, affirming as it would have that I was not matching the standard definition of male.

The summer between junior high and high school provided me with a bit of transition between the two schools. I was enrolled in summer school, and took Algebra I. What was helpful about those few intensified classes was that I got acquainted with a few students and the campus itself. When school began in September, then, I did not feel as traumatized as I had felt the first days at the other three schools I had attended since we'd arrived from Colombia. My biggest anxiety had to do with P.E. and having to shower in public. This was a greater issue now that I was having to be in a locker room with boys whose bodies looked more like men's, relative to their size and body hair.

One day I overheard a group of older boys accusing someone of being a "homo." The only time I had ever heard that word was in connection to milk. Why were they so disgusted by milk? But before you conclude that euthanasia would have been justified in my case, please realize that I was surviving life somehow, and was generally a happy person. It was the private and internal conversations with myself that were the realm of my anguish and crisis. As I stated earlier, distractions are a good thing, and, thankfully, I had plenty of things that kept me distracted for long periods of time.

As the language around me began to have more sexual connotations, I felt somewhat left out of the loop. Something inside me told me I should just go with the flow and not be asking for explanations all the time. Have you ever learned a new thing, whether it is a product, a word, or an idea, only to discover that everybody has known about it for a long time? Suddenly this "new" thing doesn't seem so new, and you feel a little foolish. That is what happened to me. Puzzled by the word "homo," which I was now hearing all over the place in a pejorative sort of tone, I asked a friend what that word meant. You should have seen the look on his face. What planet was I from, he wondered. He went on to explain that a "homo" was a man who loved men and sucked their cocks.

That was a little too much information for me, and I was disgusted by the picture it put in my head. Swear words were still seldom heard in conversations, especially the f-word. Soon curiosity got the better of me, though, and I asked yet another person what "fuck" meant. If the friend who had explained "homo" to me was incredulous, this friend was shocked that I didn't know what the word meant. I *had* to be kidding, you could practically see him thinking. Betrayed by my naiveté, I quickly figured out it was best just to pretend I knew what others were saying when they used these kinds of words.

One night in ninth grade Catechism class at the church, I had a couple of painful hangnails that were snagging on everything. I was unable to bite them off, and was thinking a pair of fingernail clippers would do the trick. The problem was that I didn't know what they were called. I turned around to ask the friend sitting behind me whether he had one of the "click-click" things, "you know, for trimming finger nails" and proceeded to show him my hangnails.

Ed, my friend, was every bit as sinister as *Eddy Haskell* on *Leave It to Beaver,* and took advantage of my lack of knowledge. He said no, he didn't have what I was after, but told me to ask the girl in sitting in front of me if she had a Kotex I could borrow. So I did. I could not figure out why she wilted forward on her desk. Ed could not contain his laughter. After class, I cornered him and insisted he tell me what a *Kotex* was, but the explanation he offered did not help clear up the matter.

"It's what girls use on their *cunts* when they have a period, you moron."

Okay, I thought, better not ask him to tell me what a "cunt" is— or what a "period" is, either.

Thankfully, that girl went to a different high school, so I only saw her at Catechism a few more times that year, and she kept her distance. That was okay with me, especially after I learned what those words meant.

Ed went to my high school, but fortunately he was so busy being himself that he never brought up my stupidity. We did have one thing in common, though: we both played the guitar. While he fancied himself as a lead singer and lead guitar player, I was content to be a rhythm guitarist, not wanting to be center stage. Along with two other friends, one who played bass and one a drummer, we formed a band.

We had a few Beatles' and Rolling Stones' songs we could play, maybe a repertoire of twenty in total, which was enough for roughly two sets. On Christmas of 1964, Ed got us our first paying gig. We were paid twenty dollars, total, to play at a college party in an apartment not far from our house. None of us was yet old enough to drive, so our parents dropped us off with all our stuff and picked us up afterwards.

The band broke up around Easter, and we each went our separate ways. Ed's ego had gotten to be too much for the rest of us, and we were not having any fun, since he was always screaming at us. The drummer, the bass player and I remained hopeful of getting together again—but without Ed.

It was a hot day in July when I got a phone call from the college student who had hired us for the Christmas party. He told me he had run into the drummer and had learned about our breakup. He wondered if I was interested in joining another band which was looking for a rhythm guitar player; that band, he told me, was having a practice the following day. I reminded him that I didn't drive, and so would likely not be able to make the rehearsal. He responded he would be more than happy to drive me to the practice. Mom, who worked part-time at I. Magnin's, was home when he called, so I told her what the call was about and got her permission to go with him the following day.

The next day he arrived as promised at 3:00 p.m., and we loaded my guitar and amplifier into the back seat of his car. As we were going down Winchester Avenue, he said he wanted to stop at his apartment for a minute. We pulled up in front of his place, and he said it was too hot to stay in the car, so why didn't I come in and cool off with a Coke? I was worried about my stuff left unattended in the car, but he said not to worry, that we would bring it into the apartment.

To cut to the chase, I was raped. Though I was not penetrated, I felt horror as he thrust his penis between my buttocks and ejaculated. And, once again, I was threatened to keep quiet. And once again I feared telling anyone for the same reasons as before. But, this time, there was the added worry that this guy knew who I was, and knew some of my friends. He used that against me when he told me he would tell my friends I was a "homo" if I said anything to anyone.

I don't need to tell you how one erects these monumental walls of protection and denial. I was somehow able to bury this horrible episode deep into my subconscious; I would not allow myself to admit that any of this had happened. This event just added to my confusion. As I was being raped, he groaned and mumbled that I was just like a girl, soft and curvy. I can still remember as if it was yesterday his whiskers on the back of my neck and cheeks as he rubbed his chin on me as he lay on top of me. It sends chills down my back as I think about it.

What was I? Why was I different? Why did these men—first the paper route customer and now this guy—single me out? What did they see in me that I didn't see in myself? I felt responsible somehow, as if I was the cause of what had happened to me. The picture was very confusing.

Puberty was now starting to affect my body. I had my first wet dream about the time of the rape; when I awoke, I thought I had wet the bed. I was devastated, because I had not wet the bed for a long time, and thought I had outgrown the problem. However, the mattress was not soaked, and the wetness was only in my undershorts. I went to the bathroom and was surprised by the slimy moist substance. I had no idea what it was. It scared me. I washed up and went back to bed. This happened a few more times, but it was not until the guy raped me that I put two and two together and realized what the fluid was. I now also realized what the man who masturbated had wiped off my hand that night. It was all too much for me. I wished this milky stuff didn't come out of me.

Chapter 8: The Power of Advertising

Given my terrible self-image and insecurities, it is ironic that I was elected as class vice-president in both my junior and senior years of high school. It had nothing to do with my being politically savvy and self-confident. On the contrary, I was horrified when I learned I had been elected. How did this happen?

Well, I was appalled at how cheesy the candidates' posters were, and, since I was an artist, I designed and silk-screened campaign posters for myself as a joke. Someone then nominated me, and I got on the ballot. Then, the morning after I attached my posters on the school's corridor walls, they were all gone! I was devastated, because I thought someone had seen through my ruse, and so had ripped them all down. It was only later that day in art class that I learned the posters had become collector's items, and students had stolen them to hang inside their lockers. I didn't even have a copy of the poster for myself! That was my first experience in the power of advertising.

Art became a sanctuary for me; one thing I could do well was draw. Art class had the reputation of being full of flunkies who needed an easy credit, but I am so glad now I took it as an elective in eleventh grade when my life needed some direction. There was a new instructor that year and, as this was her first time teaching, she was "cool." Mrs. Lozano put up with the flunkies, and had such an easy-going personality, that in a very short time she had them under control. On the other hand, she was genuinely devoted to those of us who were serious and demonstrated some ability and talent. I cannot thank her enough for the direction she provided for my life and the confidence she instilled in me as an artist.

I was fortunate to have Mrs. Lozano as a teacher for two years, and she is solely responsible for my having chosen graphic design as a career. She recommended the graphic design program at San Jose State College (now University), her alma mater.

Was I popular? I don't know. I really did not like being in the spotlight, and still had huge fears whenever I had to stand in front of the classroom to give oral reports—or for that matter, stand in front of any group. One of my fears was to mispronounce a word, and thereby sabotage my efforts to blend in and not be different. I remember once giving a book report and saying "shit" when I meant to say "sheet"—the class howled and I died a thousand deaths.

Academically, I was a "B" student. I could have done better if I had been able to focus more on my studies, but I had too much to deal with in my head. I was easily distracted by my confusing thought life. If only I could have turned off that inner voice! But I couldn't.

By eleventh grade many of my friends had girlfriends, and those who didn't were always talking about girls. I mentioned earlier in junior high school I was offended by the nasty things boys said about girls, as if they were saying them about me. The difference between those earlier comments and the ones uttered by older boys now was how they dripped with longing and an obvious lustfulness. My older brother, Enrique, had succumbed to this phenomenon and he, too, had a girlfriend. She was one of my classmates and lived not far from us. Their relationship was on and off, and I noticed Enrique was a rather jealous guy. He would swear under his breath if he ever saw her talking to another guy in a friendly way. I couldn't understand that. Even so, as time went by, I felt the pressure to have a girlfriend.

I was with my friend Mike one day, when he noticed a girl who was two years younger than us. He said she was really "hot." I watched the girl from a distance to see what it was that made him think so. She was very pretty, indeed. Mike already had a girlfriend, so in some ways this girl was off limits to him. A few days later, he told me that he had learned something that I might be interested in hearing. He told me this pretty girl had a crush on me. My head went spinning at the news. I remember feeling almost nauseous and my palms got all sweaty. These were new sensations I had never felt before. I had no idea what to do or what tactic to employ. I wasn't even sure of her name! I became tongue-tied even thinking of what to say to her, should we ever actually meet in person.

At lunchtime she would usually be with a group of two or three of her friends in the cafeteria, or out in the school plaza. I saw her stealing a look in my direction when I ventured close to her, pretending I was oblivious to her. The day arrived when we came face to face. I said "Hi,"—and then, silence. We had a brief conversation, though, and from that point on we started looking for each other. Pretty soon we were spending time or walking home together. She was a very sweet and likeable person.

The first time I held her hand I felt a mixture of elation and panic. She was so pretty it was impossible for me not to be completely taken by her. Maybe I was normal after all. I wanted it to be true.

Her name was Sherry, and she was my date for the Senior Ball. In the weeks leading up to the dance, I was driven to learn how to act like a guy. The operative word being "act." I desperately gathered intelligence from as many sources as possible. I asked Enrique a ton of questions; I tried to glean information from friends; I eavesdropped on conversations; all in an effort to know what to do and say when the day arrived. Not from a sexual point of view, but from a social perspective. I needed to know the protocols, and was determined to do the right thing. I was like an actor memorizing his part.

Doing the expected thing is a good way to fly below the radar, and I was honing my skill at doing that. But I also had an insatiable appetite for trying to figure myself out. Now much more capable in the English language, I embarked on a secret bit of research. Unfortunately, everything I unearthed made me even more unsure of what

I was. For example, when I learned the word transvestite and went to the public library to look it up, a psychology book stated it was a person who enjoyed dressing in the clothes of the opposite sex for sexual gratification. It went on to say such people were fetishistic and their behavior was considered deviant. Furthermore, it said that some individuals had been successfully treated with electroshock therapy. As fascinating and horrifying as all this sounded, I felt this description did not really describe me, since I did not cross-dress for sexual gratification. But it did make me curious about the concept, and this became a volatile mixture of ideas for me.

I never cross-dressed completely; for the most part, I only wore panties. Nor did I masturbate that often, since it produced too many strange feelings. From the first time I masturbated I experienced both ecstasy and revulsion, since it always reminded me of what that man had done years earlier with my hand wrapped around his penis. I did not like handling myself, but there was no other way to make mastur-bation happen so I learned to suppress my disdain for the moment.

Being more independent now, thanks to having a driver's li-cense and later my own car, I was able to purchase the odd "gift" for my pretend girlfriend. I also raided the clothing my mom would col-lect from time to time for the St. Vincent de Paul Society, figuring they would never be missed. The need for secrecy and the fear of being found out were indescribable. I was sure none of my friends engaged in such "deviant" behavior, and I now had another emotion to contend with—overwhelming guilt and the sense I was an awful person. How I wish I could make sense of it all. When I was younger, I prayed to God at night that the next morning I would wake up as a girl. Now I just wanted Him to make all this go away.

At church one Sunday the Gospel reading included the beauti-ful invitation made by Jesus, "Come to me, all you who are weary and heavy laden and I will give you rest..." I remember thinking how I wanted that to be true for me.

Chapter 9: The Big Bust

After graduating from high school, there was the reshuffling of relationships that happens among friends. This is when you realize you may never again see some people with whom you have spent years together. Of my graduating class of over five hundred and fifty, there were many who would be going out of state to study or moving to other college towns or cities in California. Some stayed at home in San Jose to attend the local junior colleges, colleges and universities. Only a handful of my classmates chose San Jose State, and of those I only knew three or four well enough to possibly have an on-going friendship. But of those few, given that we all had different schedules, we still almost never saw each other.

Of course, what I've described is not unique. This happens to graduating classes everywhere. Most people are able to face relocation or take a new start like this in stride. Since I was unsure of who I was, or what I was, the process for me was fraught with anxiety and trepidation. There was a sense of security in having what might be called a closed system, such as what is found from kindergarten through twelfth grade. That familiarity goes out the window upon graduating from high school. There is a period of adjustment while establishing new relationships and routines.

Perhaps the biggest adjustment for me was not the start of college and all of the changes that entailed but something quite different. A few weeks before the start of that fall semester in 1968, Enrique moved to Vancouver, B.C. to work with our brother-in-law and his father, both Canadians. Carmen had met her future husband at Foothill College and they were married in 1967. Within the year, they had moved to Canada; this was the start of our family's migration to yet another new country. When Enrique left San Jose I lost my role model. He was the person to whom I looked for examples of how to act, what to say, and how to navigate through life. I can say all of this, and really only in retrospect, because at the time I didn't realize what a huge void his departure would create in my world.

Slowly the temperature was rising in this pressure cooker that was my life. I desperately needed answers to my questions, but I did not know what exactly to ask, or where to look for the answers. I felt so young, immature and inexperienced—and I was, in fact, all of these. I was still seventeen years old when I graduated from high school and wouldn't turn eighteen until my first semester in college. As I looked around the classrooms, which included students of all ages, I was sure I was the youngest person in the room.

By coincidence, I recognized one individual in more than one of my classes that first semester. We started a casual friendship, and I soon learned that Bruce was a veteran going to school on the G.I. Bill. He was about twenty-six years old, and had a calm, laid-back air about him. Perhaps he took pity on me, or recognized my vulnerability, but he was very kind and friendly toward me. I envied his sense of quiet confidence, and wished I had a small measure of it for myself.

I cannot remember the rest of the conversation or how it started, but Bruce suggested I might be interested in reading a book titled *Siddhartha*, by Hermann Hesse. He told me I would find it in the college bookstore, and highly recommended it. I devoured that book faster than any other book I'd ever read in my life. Even though the book did nothing to solve my issues, it opened my mind to the possibility that I might be able to overcome them by transcending them somehow.

Life is complicated at the best of times, and with the war in Vietnam in full swing, the political unrest on campuses, and the anti-establishment mentality all around me, I needed something—and I needed it soon. This idea of simplicity in life and the quest for inner peace came at the right time for me.

In the months that followed, as college life began to fall into place for me, I was drawn to those people who seemed to exhibit the same qualities I saw in Bruce. I had stopped attending the Catholic Church by then, and had lost any hope of finding meaning in what I knew—though I realize now, I knew very little. I began delving into Eastern philosophies because I so desperately needed something to identify with—or to give me an identity—and these seemed to provide it. I was still living at home, and, though I didn't realize it at the time, this new phase I was going through was causing me to rethink all of my relationships, including those with my family.

Sadly, it was about this time my grandmother was diagnosed with cancer. She died in the spring of the following year after a painful battle. Life at home was now very different: my two older siblings, Carmen and Enrique, now lived in Canada, and my grandmother was no longer with us. I was now the oldest child at home. But I needed to break those bonds, and this made no sense to my parents. They must have perceived me as some self-righteous, anti-everything ingrate person.

With respect to my "gender identity" (which is not how I thought of it then), I had gone through several episodes of collecting a few female garments—and then purging them out of my life. One day my mom decided to reorganize my closet, and found a jacket that I seldom wore with its sleeves stuffed full of some things I had collected. I was downstairs in the family room. Everybody was home. She came to the top of the stairwell and called for both my dad and me to come upstairs immediately. Imagine my horror when I came into my room and saw all these things piled on top of my bed. Dad walked in right behind me and saw the same thing. Mom demanded an explanation. I saw my life flash before my eyes. As I thought to myself that finally my secret was out, I heard another part of my brain begin to articulate this ridiculous story about a panty raid at one of the college dorms.

Since I was the one who had the car, I said, after the raid I had gotten stuck with the bounty, and was only hiding it because I didn't know what else to do with it. I didn't want to throw it away, because I thought that would be a waste and a crime.

I don't know how convincing I was, but both of them walked out of my bedroom, with mom muttering something about placing the garments in a Goodwill box, since it would now be impossible to return them to their proper owners. I'd dodged another bullet. I had no alternative but to purge one more time, and I felt horrible about it. But I also felt that I had missed a chance to pour my heart out to my parents about what I had been going through all my life. Yet I was convinced that had I done so, they would not have been able to deal with or understand it.

It wouldn't be long before I would begin a new collection of clothes, with new hiding places, and new tactics to ensure this would never happen again. I needed to move out; of this I was convinced now more than ever. But I couldn't afford to; first, I needed to find a job that would allow me to pay rent and other living expenses.

At the time steak-and-lobster restaurants were the new craze, and there was a new such location not far from home. This particular restaurant was very busy, so I applied for a job, and was hired as a bus boy. Though it only paid three dollars an hour, once the tips were added, it provided me with enough money to pay for gas and car insurance. But it was not enough to cover rent.

After about six months of working as a busboy there was an opening in the kitchen for a meat cutter. The head chef had been doing the meat cutting along with all his duties and responsibilities, and it was getting to be too much for him. I was promoted and trained by him to trim and cut the top sirloin butts, as well as New York strip loins and tenderloins into various portion sizes with speed and accuracy. There was a quota that had to be cut for each day of the week, but the great thing about the job was as long as it got done by 3:00 p.m., I could come in at any time to do it. The other great thing was I could grow my hair long, which was not permitted if working in the dining room. I would come in at 5:00 a.m., do my job, and be gone on most days before 7:30 a.m.

Though I no longer qualified for tips, I was getting paid considerably more per hour than I had been as a bus boy, and this finally afforded me the chance to move out. It was a very emotional day for my mom when I came with a friend's VW van to move my belongings. Through Bruce I had found a room in a house near the campus, where the rent was very reasonable. When Bruce told me about this house, he warned me one of the other tenants was a "Jesus freak." I remember thinking to myself I was cool with this since I, too, was "spiritual," so I was unfazed by the news.

The Jesus freak's name was Dennis, and his older brother, Roger, also lived in this house. The house was actually owned by their father, who had purchased it as revenue property when Roger started as a student at San Jose State a few years earlier. Dennis was a year younger than me, but what bothered me about him was not that he was a Jesus freak, but that he seemed to exude a peace and confidence I didn't possess. It wouldn't be long before I would experience his evangelistic fervor first-hand, which was always peppered with Bible verses: some I recognized, but most were foreign to me. The fact was I had never picked up a Bible to read it for myself; only what I heard during the Catholic Mass formed my then Christian understanding.

Chapter 10: What Do I Know?

Dennis was not the only Jesus freak I saw around; they seemed to be coming out of the woodwork! They were all over campus. Their appearance was a mixture of hippie and surfer: long hair, beads, sandals and tie-dyed T-shirts. But I must say every encounter I had with them, or any chance I had to overhear their conversations, always left me thinking I wanted what they were talking about for myself.

One of the things that impressed me about Dennis, and that also came as complete surprise to me, was that he was a conscientious objector and was, therefore, exempt from the draft. I knew of several denominations and religions that automatically entitled one to be classified as a conscientious objector, but Dennis did not belong to any of these. This piqued my curiosity, and I asked him a lot of questions about it, because I knew at least three other people who had applied for this deferment and had been rejected. I needed to know what it was Dennis had said that made the difference in his case.

His answer both puzzled and intrigued me. He claimed that he simply explained to the panel interviewing him his beliefs based on several Bible verses and that he'd been able to defend his position to their satisfaction.

On one level, I felt I was no less spiritual than Dennis, and so thought that I, too, should have a conscientious objector deferment, instead of simply what I had since turning eighteen, which was a student deferment. I sought out other friends of mine who had not qualified for the sort of deferment Dennis had obtained, and asked them what their experiences had been. They all told me that it was not easy to convince the panel. I learned that the interview was designed to challenge you to defend your beliefs. It was very intimidating, insofar as if you claimed that you were a Buddhist, they would have Buddhist priests and scholars doing the interview. If you claimed to be a Christian, they would have ministers or priests asking you questions. It didn't matter your philosophy or religious affiliation; they had people well versed in whatever anyone claimed to be or believe.

What chance could I possibly have?

Nevertheless, one day I drove to the draft board, and walked in to apply for the conscientious objector deferment. The lady behind the counter explained that first I needed to fill out some forms and bring them back. After the forms were received I would receive the official application, and, once the application was accepted, then I would be called in for an interview.

When I got home I put the form on top of my desk and went off to one of my afternoon art classes. Later that night I sat at the desk, and filled out the top portion of the form, which included name, address, selective service number and other "administrivial" questions. Then there were the four questions asked on the form. I decided to write out my answers on binder paper first, and then copy them to the form.

The first question was, "What is the basis for your belief that war is wrong?" Next was a question about what books I had read, or who had influenced me, to come to the beliefs I had; I was asked to list pertinent references. The third question simply asked whether, based on my beliefs, I would be able to participate in the military in a non-combatant status, such as a medic or materials handling, etc.

The final question asked if I had ever publicly or privately, written or orally, expressed my views; it asked me to cite places, dates and times of such declarations.

It seemed simple enough. I started with the first question by answering, "The basis for my belief that war is wrong is..." and proceeded to write almost two pages of my beliefs—a mishmash of Christian, Eastern philosophy, and my own personal ideas and thoughts. I stopped to review what I had written, glanced back at the form and saw the four lines I had available in which to answer the question. I looked back at my long answer, then back at the form—then it dawned on me I should be able to answer this crucial question in only four lines. I crumpled up my two sheets of paper and threw them into the trash can, starting over again.

I could not get beyond the words 'the basis for my belief is...' I could not answer the question, and as I sat there, my beliefs unraveled. It was like taking an onion and peeling off layer after layer as I asked myself what it was I really believed. Was I really a conscientious objector, or was I doing this simply to satisfy my self-righteous spiritual view of who I was? I could not with any certainty claim any one belief system, because I would not have been able to defend such a position to anyone. And in those honest moments, I admitted the only reason I was against war was not because I had any moral qualms about pulling a trigger in a justified war, but only because I did not want to die. And why didn't I want to die? Because I did not know if there was a God, or if there was a heaven or a hell. But that kind of answer would not have satisfied the Draft Board.

In my confusion about what I was and the distress it caused me, I had often thought about death. At times I felt I just could not go on, and that death would be better than continuing on with my confusion and despair. What kept me from going there was always this nagging issue of whether there was more to life than what I could see. What if there was a heaven? What if there was a hell? I remember directing the voice in my head to God, and saying that if He was responsible for the things I admired in Dennis, then I would also like those things for myself. But at the same time I was having bad thoughts, there was another voice that challenged the notion altogether: how do I know if there even is a God?

I never did get a conscientious objector deferment; I did not need one. Nixon was winding down the war in Vietnam and the U.S. Army was not drafting as many individuals. Eventually, the draft system was changed to a lottery based on date of birth; and after the first year of this new system, I was reclassified as 1H. I was no longer in danger of getting drafted.

An interesting thing began to happen in my life soon after this. I sensed something different about my perspective on life and on myself. In many ways, I found this most liberating. I did not know what was going on, but, thanks to the psychology course I was enrolled in that semester, I feared I might be schizophrenic, or worse. I sure seemed to fit some of the definitions I'd learned. Yet there was this undeniable sense of tranquility that I was experiencing for the first time in my life. I did not tell anyone what was going through my head, and I especially did not want to be thought of as a Jesus freak. I could hear the kind of mocking and ridicule Dennis endured from everyone, including from his older brother.

One of the differences I noticed almost immediately was the ease with which I was able to have conversations with girls. This was new to me, because I always felt tongue-tied; I always seemed to lack the script for what I should say. I felt this crazy pressure to befriend girls in order to get them into bed. At least that was my view of how the guys I knew always seemed to think. But it was not how I felt. Suddenly I found myself having amazingly friendly conversations without any hidden agenda or motivation on my part—conversations about stuff in class, about events, about everything. Often after a conversation like this, I would think to myself, "Wow, I was just talking to a girl! And I wasn't at all choked up!"

Another change had to do with my consumption of beer, wine and the occasional joint, finding myself shying away from these. This had nothing to do with my having formed some kind of ideology or legalistic outlook; I just simply didn't feel like getting drunk and stoned anymore.

One Friday night at a party I arrived with my usual six-pack of beer, popped one open, and stood in the kitchen with several friends who were passing a joint around. Whenever the joint came to me, I would simply pass it to the next person without thinking. The can of beer I was holding in my hand was still full after quite a while; I was hardly sipping from it. Suddenly one of the guys in the circle screamed at me.

"What the fuck is wrong with you, Salazar?" he said. "Did you get religion?" All the other guys standing there seemed to agree with his sentiment.

I emphatically denied the allegation; but it left me flabbergasted. Not once had I espoused or mentioned anything about what was going through my head during those days. I had deliberately kept my mouth shut; the last thing I wanted was to lose friends or to be rejected. My new "unconscious" behavior had, in a sense, betrayed me. The changes I thought were internal and private were somehow apparent to others after all.

Chapter 11: Spiritual War

The night I was suspected of having "gotten religion" I walked home with my guitar—and my remaining beers—feeling somewhat dejected, but elated at the same time. I was dejected because these guys, whom I thought were friends, had rejected me. I thought I knew them better, but I realized our relationships were solely based on getting stoned and drinking beer; they didn't care for me as a person. And, to be honest, there were things about them I didn't like; I didn't really care for them, either. But I was elated, because there was something liberating taking place within me, and that helped to overcome this rejection.

For several weeks I kept my mouth shut, but now there was no denying it. The words I overheard Dennis and the other Jesus-freaks speaking resonated deep within me. I was comforted by their message and inspired by their faith. One night I finally worked up the courage to knock on Dennis' bedroom door. He was surprised to see me, and asked what I wanted. Looking nervously around to make sure no one had seen me, I told him I needed to talk to him about something.

He invited me in, and asked me to have a seat on one of the two chairs in his room; he sat on the other. Not knowing where to begin, I started by telling him that for several weeks I thought maybe I had been losing my mind. I shared with him about the night I had come to realize I didn't want to die until I knew if Jesus was real, and whether or not there is a heaven or hell. I then explained how I was noticing some new and different things in my life ever since then. Without saying anything about my secrets, I added that I was also aware of what I was like before I started noticing these changes.

The look on his face made me think that maybe I had said too much; but he was very sympathetic when he asked me if I could elaborate. I told him about the night of the party when I had been accused of being religious, how I felt embarrassed and unwanted, but I also felt elated and was genuinely happy about what had happened. I told him I had been trying to make sense of all of this, and based on some of my recent lectures in psychology, the duality I was noticing in me seemed too much like schizophrenia. In essence, that was all I could say.

Dennis asked if he could read something to me from the Bible. I said yes, and he read this verse to me from Paul's second letter to the church in Corinth, chapter 5, and verse 17.

> "Therefore if anyone is in Christ, he is a new creature; the old things passed away; behold, new things have come. Now all these things are from God..."

I asked him to read it again, and sat thinking to myself that this made a lot of sense. It helped explain this duality I was very much aware of—the way I felt like a new person compared to the old person I had been. I asked him if what I had been going through meant I was 'in Christ?'

His response was warm and genuine, "It sounds like it to me."

The next day he presented me with an extra King James Bible he had in his room. The edges of the pages were red, the pages yellowed. It must have been an old pew Bible from some church. I had never owned a Bible in my life, or read one seriously. He told me I should read the Gospel of John and try to stick to the New Testament for now. Honestly speaking, I had a difficult time with the King's English and found reading the Bible difficult. But I didn't know there were newer translations that used modern English.

It might have been later that day that Dennis asked if I'd like to go to one of the Bible studies he attended. This was all happening too fast, I thought. As it turned out, there was a scheduling conflict, and I was not going to be able to attend the study with him. That bought me some time. A few days later Dennis asked if I wanted to go to church with him on Sunday. I agreed to.

Prior to this, I'd only been inside a Protestant church twice in my life: once for a wedding, and once for a funeral.

The church Dennis and I attended that Sunday morning was a small Pentecostal church near the campus. I found the whole experience unsettling. I had never heard what they called "speaking in tongues," and was very self-conscious about raising my hands in the air with everyone else. However, I was really impressed with how full the church was with people my age. There was a lot of singing, and it was loud. This was also new to me, because singing at the Catholic Church where I grew up was subdued in comparison. I also found it interesting that this congregation was somehow affiliated to a Pentecostal church in Vancouver, where my sister Carmen and brother Enrique now lived.

Meeting new people and making new starts had always been difficult for me, and though it was no different that morning, I felt welcomed and was received warmly by complete and total strangers.

Back at the restaurant where I worked, I had developed a friendship with the chef, John, and he often told me to come and hang out on the weekends in nearby Campbell, where he, his wife and two young daughters lived in a rented farmhouse. Actually, it was John who loaned me the VW van I had used for my move. John was a trained chef, but he was very hip, with longish hair and a short beard and always wore leather sandals when not at work. I liked him a lot. I always had this sense he could read into my soul, that he knew about my gender confusion. He didn't, of course; he never knew or suspected anything. But John was the first person I ever came close to actually telling my secret; I felt very safe with him and his wife.

I was not the only person to whom John had given an open invitation to hang out at his house. The fact was many people used to show up on the weekends, and it was not uncommon for musicians to bring their guitars and other instruments. We used to sing a lot of Joni Mitchell, Judy Collins, Gordon Lightfoot, and Bob Dylan songs.

One very talented person, who sometimes switched between playing bass and banjo, remarked one day he had heard a new band called "Love Song," and asked me if I'd ever heard of them. He was really impressed by them. Not only were they good musicians, he said, but they also had amazing harmonies. But what intrigued him the most was that they were a "Jesus" band. I had never heard of such a thing, and was naturally curious. This "Jesus" thing seemed to be everywhere!

Within walking distance of San Jose State was the small campus of San Jose Bible College. We had heard about an open-air concert that was going to be held on an upcoming Saturday, which I attended with Dennis and some of his friends. When we arrived, the place was packed; there was music in the air, and overall a very festive atmosphere. It was a real "love-in" without the drugs, alcohol and "free love" I had seen in rock concerts at the county fairgrounds or on campus.

More importantly, through these first few weeks and months of my new Christian experience, I had come to believe and hope I was going to be made normal and that all my confusion and anxiety about my gender was going to be removed. In this new way of looking at things, I began to develop a very fundamentalist view of life with very well defined boundaries and codes of behavior. This fervor was not only stimulated by the sermons and devotionals I was hearing, but also by several books that were very popular with Christians at the time. One of them was *The Late Great Planet Earth* by Hal Lindsey, and his book that followed, *Satan Is Alive And Well On The Planet Earth*. Thus began my practice to spiritualize my condition, and to deal with it as if it were a spiritual problem in a war to be fought against the devil.

Chapter 12: Stupid Zeal

I mentioned that the day I moved out of the house had been emotional for my mom. I realize now what she was going through. Her mother was gone, her oldest daughter and son were in a different country, and now I was moving out, too. All the sacrifice and all the hard work she and my father had done in order to make our life better must have tasted like ashes in her mouth that day. This six-bedroom house they had so lovingly purchased and customized for us—including the addition of a built-in backyard swimming pool—now seemed empty, with no one in three of its bedrooms.

By this time my parents had invested in their own business, and operated a dry-cleaning plant in one of the many malls of West San Jose. The idea had originally been to be the owner-manager and to have the qualified staff do all the work. Because of the laws governing dry cleaners, dad needed someone with a valid boiler license to operate the steam equipment. He was able to find an older gentleman through the dry cleaners' union, as well as a couple of women who could do the pressing. He and my mother took turns working the counter and mom also offered her alteration services. Things seem to be off to a good start until the day the man hired to do the dry-cleaning almost lost his hand when he failed to apply the brake to the large cleaning machine. He began to empty the drum when the load shifted and his hand got caught between the opening and the door. Dad was forced to learn how to operate the equipment as quickly as possible and had to pass the test in order to be certified to operate the boiler. Finding a replacement for this man was impossible, so this became my dad's full-time job, instead of being just the owner-manager. I admire my dad and mom for what they had to do for us; they did it willingly and gladly.

It also pains me to admit that in my newfound excitement and zeal about my faith I failed to show them true love. In a self-righteous display of superiority, I came home one night to proclaim I had become a Christian. I walked in carrying the King James Bible that Dennis had given me, and accused the Roman Catholic Church of hypocrisy, and, by implication, my parents as well. They were hurt and their reaction validated me in a bizarre sort of way. I accused them of being like the self-righteous Pharisees Jesus often confronted, when, in fact, I was the one being self-righteous! I was so wrong to have done that to them.

In defense, mom challenged me and said if what I had was real and if I really felt the Roman Catholic Church was so wrong, then I had an obligation not to judge it but to come back to the Catholic Church and to work from within to effect change. I scoffed at the idea. Why would I want to come back to such blatant bigotry? She pointed out how one's responsibility is always first to family and then to the world; by extension, the Catholic Church was my family.

I left the house angry that night. Instead of my parents having been excited for me, they were skeptical. They said they had seen me go through many phases in the last few years, and perhaps this was just another one. Mom also wanted me to speak to a priest.

My new faith also caused me to do something about my small collection of girl's clothing. I felt guilty for having these things, so I purged them all. I saw them as tools of the devil to trap me. I was resolute on never buying girl's clothing again; to do so was sinful, it was also depraved. All the horrible things I had read in those psychology textbooks added to my zeal and fervor. I was determined to become normal with God's help.

It was also about this time that Enrique changed jobs in Vancouver. He was no longer working for our brother-in-law; he had been hired by a large heavy equipment dealer to work in their marketing department designing brochures and other promotional materials. Though he was not a trained graphic designer, he was a very talented draftsman and a quick study when it came to visual projects. He took advantage of his interaction with the printing companies that serviced the company he worked for, asked a lot of questions, and got a lot of tips from their production artists. He also researched as much as he could about typography, and how to specify and order type. The few times he returned to California, such as for our parents anniversary or for Christmas, we would talk about graphic design, and he was jealous of me because I was studying what he wished he had himself. I thought it was interesting and ironic how he was now looking at me for direction, instead of the other way around.

All this talk about graphic design got Enrique really excited and he became convinced that if I moved up to Vancouver, we could form a small company to offer graphic design services. Initially I thought he was crazy. Why would I want to go up to Vancouver? For one, on the two occasions I had come up to visit him and Carmen, the weather had been cloudy and cold—in summer! Second, I had this aversion to new starts, and, to be honest, this one frightened me.

But the reality was that if I was going to pursue graphic design as a career, I was going to have to move to a larger, more commercial center. Graphic design jobs in San Jose were limited to working in newspapers or small printing companies, as there were few advertising agencies there at the time. The computer revolution and all of the creative services it would spawn were still a decade away. San Francisco was one option and Los Angeles was another if I was going to stay in California. The idea of moving to a city where I knew no one was not an choice I was prepared to consider. Suddenly my brother's crazy idea of moving up to Vancouver seemed logical. So we were actually already making plans and dreaming of how this would happen when I came into this new spiritual part of my journey.

One night, at the Bible study I was now attending near campus, the man who taught the lesson asked anyone with a prayer request to see him afterwards. Nervously, I waited my turn and I asked him to pray for my family and explained how I had a confrontation with my parents, more specifically with my mother. I shared her comments and how she challenged me to come back to the Catholic Church. She said this would demonstrate to her what I had was real and not just another phase I was going through.

His answer surprised me. He agreed with my mother, and said if what I had was true and genuine, then I should be willing to go back so she could see the changes were genuine. This is not what I wanted to hear; I wanted him to feel sorry for me, and to agree with me, not with them. But I was also humbled, and concluded that I did want my mom to see I was being sincere, and that what I had found was real.

The night I had the argument with my mom about my *new* faith, one of the points I made had to do with music and how fervently from the heart Jesus people sang at church. She had countered that I needed to attend the new Sunday evening "Folk Mass," which was for young people. Feeling admonished by what the Bible study leader said to me, I decided to attend this *folk* Mass that following Sunday.

What I can only describe as heartbreak is what I felt when I went to that Mass. Yes, there was singing, but the only people singing with any conviction were the eight or so individuals who were leading at the front of the church. I wondered if the music was simply like the proverbial spoonful of sugar to help the medicine go down. I was moved, and realized here were all these people who just seemed to be going through the motions, but for whom their faith was simply something they did out of obligation and habit, and not from the heart. It reminded me of how I had felt in church years earlier.

The priest who said the Mass that night had been at the parish for several years, I recognized him—Father Maguire. At the end of the service he came to the back of the church to greet people on their way out. I waited until the church was almost empty before I approached him. He remembered me after all these years. His sincerity was unquestionable. When I told him I had been "born again," his response was another surprise. He was very excited and happy for me. He thought it was great!

I had been thinking about what possible involvement I might have back at this parish. I offered to volunteer to work with the high school group, said I had learned some Christian songs, and could also possibly help out during the Mass. This pleased him greatly, and he asked me if I remembered the McLaughlins.

Of course I remembered them. They were the couple who had taught the weekly catechism class to junior high school students way back when. I just hoped they didn't remember me, or at least not my ignorant answer about the facts of life! Father Maguire informed me they ran the high school Catechism class which met once a month at one of the local monasteries for a one-day retreat. He said they would be very happy to have me help them in any way possible, and announced that they, too, were "born-again."

In my mind I thought, "Wait a minute, what's going on?" But this excited me as much as it excited the priest that night. It wasn't long before I met with this couple, and then the other adult volunteers who helped with the high school group. I attended their first retreat in November, which was held in a monastery near Stanford University. It was a beautiful setting deep in the woods; years earlier it had been a seminary. However, now the priesthood was not attracting as many into its ranks and the buildings had been virtually mothballed. The monastery was now used for retreats and conferences.

The high school retreats worked as follows: students would meet at the church on Sunday at 1 P.M. and then be driven by volunteer parents and drivers to the monastery, where there would be some activity, followed by a short devotional and discussion, then by a Mass, and finally a meal. They were back at the church by 6 P.M. to be picked up by their parents.

For the upcoming December retreat, which was to take place during their Christmas vacation, we wanted to do something special. A man who attended a Protestant church in the neighborhood had been given permission to lead a non-denominational Bible study on Wednesday evenings at the church. I had been asked to investigate this Bible study to see if it would be suitable for us to direct high school students there who might be interested in such a study. I had gone a couple of times, and found it to be simply wonderful. The man was a layman with an impressive knowledge of the Bible, and was sensitive to the doctrinal differences that sometimes divide Catholics and Protestants. He made certain anyone who came, whether Catholic or Protestant, was welcome. The McLaughlins suggested perhaps Stewart might know a half dozen or so young Jesus People who could come and share what Jesus meant to them, with the hope that this might challenge the high school students who attended.

Stewart was more than happy to help us with this request and invited six people for that Sunday. We all met at the church at the designated time, and I was asked to stay behind and wait for any late-comers. I waited an additional fifteen minutes and just as I was driving away I saw a young woman trying the locked doors of the church. I assumed she might be one of the high school students, or one of the guests who had been invited. I rolled down the window to ask if she was looking for the group. I told her they had already left, that I was designated to drive anybody who arrived late. I asked her if she wanted to ride with me to the monastery.

She accepted my offer, and off we went to Palo Alto. Along the way we talked about this and that, and how she knew Stewart. She told me a bit about the group of Jesus People she was part of. Some of them attended Stewart's church, but the majority, including her, went to other churches in the area.

That December retreat was a confirmation to me God was working in my life, because the indignation I had felt towards the Catholic Church had evaporated. I felt a real and genuine love for the students, and a bond of brotherhood with the McLaughlins and with the priests at the parish.

Almost three months had passed since that night in Dennis' room when I had come to a deeper faith in Jesus. And for those three months I had been free of the identity torment. This is not to say I was not aware of my issues, it is just I was so absolutely determined to be "victorious" in this spiritual battle that I spent my energy convincing myself I was going to be healed. If I allowed myself to fail, it would be a sign of my lack of faith. I had to prove to myself, and others, that I had an unshakable faith. Period.

The Wednesday night Bible study led by Stew became my main source of spiritual sustenance and of deep friendships for the year that followed, until I moved to Canada.

Chapter 13: We Meet Again

On the Thursday after the retreat I went to the restaurant where I worked to collect my paycheck and tips. The parking lot was full when I arrived so I had to park a fair distance from the door. As I was walking towards the entrance, four young women in nurse's white uniforms came out of the restaurant, I recognized one of them as the girl I had given a ride from the church to the retreat. I could see she was visibly upset about something; I could see that she also was a little embarrassed for me to see her in such a state. I asked her if everything was okay.

It became obvious she didn't feel free to talk in front of her friends, so I offered to drive her back to the office where she worked. She accepted my offer. I told her I would be right back, then dashed into the restaurant, picked up my check, returned to the car, and drove her back to work. Her name was Rachel, and I learned a little bit more about her on the way back to her office.

She actually worked for an oral surgeon, and was upset because the other nurses had been making fun of her for what they thought were old-fashioned views on marriage. When we got to her office she asked me if I would like to come to her apartment for a spaghetti dinner with some of her friends on Friday night. I accepted, got directions to her apartment, and we said goodbye.

Rachel lived with three girlfriends, all part of a larger group of Christian young people who attended a Bible study every Tuesday night. I got to meet her friends and some of the other people who came that night. I felt right at home with all of them. I had found a group with whom I had a lot in common, not just in terms of age but also beliefs. The Tuesday night Bible study was held in a couple's converted garage; it were known as the Wallace's. Mr. Wallace and his wife were teachers in their fifties, but they knew how to relate to this disparate group of young people from all kinds of backgrounds. It was a beautiful demonstration, I thought to myself, of what the early church must have been like. There was a genuine and wholesome love and care for each other, and lives were being changed before our eyes. Druggies were going straight and previously wild, irresponsible behavior was being tempered and transformed into its antithesis. This was a huge contrast to the parties I had been going to where getting drunk and stoned was the objective.

I think the most obvious change in my life was my taste in music. Funny how so many of the songs I knew no longer gave me the same kind of pleasure I had enjoyed from them before. They seemed so artificial and "carnal" and it was difficult for me to sing them now with any kind of conviction or seriousness. I was really motivated to learn some of the new Christian songs I was hearing at the time. I don't think this genre had yet been labeled as "contemporary Christian music;" these songs were just starting to become popular and accepted in some of the more progressive churches.

Back at my parish, I had started to lead the singing at the twelve o'clock Mass, which was the least attended on Sunday. My previous fear of being in front of a large group was suddenly gone—at least when I was in church. I never in my wildest dreams imagined it would seem so easy for me to do this.

Changes were also taking place within the Roman Catholic Church; the fact a non-denominational Bible study led by a Protestant was allowed on its property was proof of this. Sometime in the spring of 1972, the McLaughlins told me the parish council had approved a motion to send me to attend an international youth conference in Dallas sponsored by Campus Crusade for Christ called "Explo '72." It was to be held that June. I had not even heard of it when they told me. LIFE magazine would later report this event with a picture on the front cover, accompanied by the headline, "The Great Jesus Rally in Dallas." I was given a brochure, and told the parish was covering my airfare and expenses, since I would be going as the parish's delegate. I was overwhelmed and grateful for the honor.

On the following Tuesday at the Wallace's Bible study, Rachel made an announcement and said her father lived in the Dallas-Fort Worth area and that he would welcome anyone who needed a place to stay in case they were going to Explo '72. I spoke to her after the Bible study and told her I was going, and the church was paying for the airfare and registration, but we had not yet made arrangements for accommodations. I continued if it were possible to stay with her father this would be most appreciated. Rachel was going to be there herself, not just for this youth event, but to visit her sisters for a couple of weeks.

You've heard the phrase, "the higher they climb, the farther they fall." Well, that's what happened to me about that time, as well. I had been so "good" about my secret for months and had resisted temptation to give in to my needs. Then one afternoon it happened. My younger sister, Angela discovered one of her bras in my room, stashed behind a box of LPs. She had come in to borrow a couple of records, which was perfectly okay with me. I was in the room at the time and she picked up the bra and asked me what it was doing there.

Not only was I busted by my sister, I felt I had betrayed and insulted God. I felt horrible. Once again my brain kicked into survival mode and I made up some story about just having been curious to see what the bra felt like, nothing more. I told her I thought every guy on the planet had probably done something similar and I made light of it. I begged her to please not tell anyone and she told me not to worry about it. She knew guys who did this kind of stuff and left it at that.

How could I possibly still be afflicted by whatever it was that made me feel and act this way? Why wasn't God fixing it? What was it going to take? Was my faith really that weak?

With respect to my planned move to Canada, I had concluded that in order to make my departure not so emotional and difficult, it would be best for me not to get too close to people. I had already experienced what that was like when we left Colombia, and I knew I was not strong enough to go through that again. That is not to say my relationships with these new friends was cold and distant; it is just that I tried to keep them in perspective and did not allow myself to think of anyone in any other way than simply brothers and sisters in Christ. This was tremendously helpful when it came to my relationships with the girls in the group, because I had no ulterior motives or hidden agendas; after all, they were my "sisters." The result was I developed very platonic relationships, particularly with Rachel. So while we did things together, like going to the beach or driving into the Santa Cruz Mountains, we never perceived these outings as *dates*. Maybe we were fooling ourselves, but that is what it was, simply two friends enjoying each other's company with a common bond, which was our faith.

I finished my studies that year, and graduated from San Jose State College. I was part of the first graduating class from the now-renamed San Jose State University. As Ronald Reagan was the governor at the time, his signature was on my diploma.

June came and off I went to Dallas. I was picked up at the airport by Rachel and her father, and driven back to her dad's apartment. Rachel stayed with one of her two sisters. I got to meet her family that week; little did I know I would be getting married to Rachel two years later. But this was the furthest thing from my mind at that time. In retrospect, I have concluded that, though I was clueless at the time, events in my life were being orchestrated on my behalf by God's hand. I could not have planned any of it.

As I grew in my faith, a little humbler now thanks to my indiscretion, I continued to believe someday I was going to be normal. The process was not going to be overnight, and it was going to require my complete dedication, self-discipline and a willingness to lay down my life on a moment-by-moment basis if I was ever going to get rid of this awful thing and win the battle.

I never shared with anyone about my secret. I had come to embrace the promise that once we confess our sins, our sins were washed away, as far removed from us as east is from west; God did not remember them anymore. How wonderful, I thought. If God was not holding them against me, then I didn't need to tell anyone about them.

Chapter 14: Fundamentally Speaking

My knowledge of the Bible was growing slowly; I was particularly interested in any verses or passages that might offer me the support I needed to maintain my "sobriety." These new tools were put to use and I was continually flogging myself with them in order to drive this demon out of my life.

The relentless and persistent way in which I would find myself thinking and dwelling on my issue made me feel all the more guilty and weak. But I zealously devoted myself to this uphill battle, all the while keeping it to myself.

In conversations with Enrique in Vancouver, we had talked about my making the move in 1973. I wanted to take a year off before I started working full-time as a graphic designer. The restaurant I worked for had merged with several other restaurants, and this new company had plans for expansion across the United States. I had a good relationship with the owners, and I was now working as a waiter making way more money than I had previously as a meat cutter, thanks to the tips.

Additionally, they were hiring me to design menus and announcements for the company. Because of the experience I had working on the floor and in the kitchen, and now with the marketing group, they offered me a full-time job if I went into their management-training program. I declined, since my plans were to be in Canada within a year. Also, though I didn't say this, I did not want to be living out of a suitcase all over the United States, since the job entailed being part of an opening team at new locations.

Nevertheless, the work I was doing for them as a waiter and as a graphic designer was just right for me at the time, since I had plenty of free time on my hands for church related activities.

There was much talk among some of my Christian friends, including Stewart, the man who led the Bible study at the Catholic Church, about a Bible teacher who offered a one-week seminar known as *Basic Youth Conflicts*. Bill Gothard was a very conservative and fundamentalist lay-teacher who had developed a curriculum he employed in his work with young people in Chicago. His work was touted as being grounded in the Bible, and much needed to counteract deteriorating family and social values.

Many evangelical churches in the San Francisco Bay area were planning to send large groups of their members to attend an upcoming seminar that was held in San Francisco's Cow Palace. It was a five-day event in the evenings. I was one of the many who attended the Wallace's group who signed up to attend a seminar.

It was exactly the kind of teaching I felt I needed in order to be victorious. I hoped that as my faith grew, so would my sense of being normal. Much of the seminar dealt with issues that constituted a positive self-image in light of God's truth, abstinence from premarital sex, God's ideal plan for marriage, Bible memorization, and many other such issues. I welcomed all of it with gusto.

But I was also aware that not all church-going people felt this seminar series was balanced when it came to its views on the role of women in the church and in society. According to the seminar teacher, women were to be subservient and submissive to men, and should not be in leadership over men. Perhaps it is not fair for me to make gross generalizations one way or another; I just want to give you a sense of the fundamentalist nature of what was taught.

The problem with learning so many new rules and doctrines is I couldn't help but begin to apply them if I was to derive any of the promised benefits. Basically, I approached all of this from a very cause-and-effect point of view. If I want to be like this, I would have to do that first. If I ever failed at something, there was a sense of going back to square one to see what I had missed so it would not happen again.

Nagging questions and feelings of inadequacy as a male were always there. The reminder that something unwanted was still part of me was no further than the bathroom. Assuming the average person empties their bladders a minimum of four or five times a day, for me, each of those nature calls was a visual reminder of so much that troubled me.

I have concluded, when God told Abraham he and his male descendants were to circumcise themselves as a sign of the covenant, He was asking them to do this for this very reason. Knowing these people would need to have a constant reminder they were covenanted, He commanded them to be circumcised. In this way they would be reminded of the covenant every time they handled themselves, on an average of four or five times a day. Very clever of God, wouldn't you say?

The way I tried to deal with this tension was by telling myself it was okay, God knew I was weak, and I just had to be patient because all this was going to go away one day.

Up in Vancouver, Enrique was thinking the large company he worked for might need a second graphic designer to help with the workload that was increasing all the time. He put pressure on me to prepare my portfolio and to send it to him as soon as it was ready. It took me several weeks to collect and mount a sufficient number of pieces to include.

I engineered a cardboard and Styrofoam case to protect the contents and shipped the portfolio. He received it within a couple of days and immediately took it to work to show his boss. His boss was very impressed with the portfolio, but explained to Enrique that the company did not want to expand its marketing department at that time. Enrique's plan for me to work there with him fizzled.

That very same day, his boss had been invited to lunch by the president of a printing company. The printer explained that his company could not only look after their printing needs, but would soon be able to assist with some of their creative needs as well, because they were setting up an in-house graphic design office. When my brother's boss asked the printer if he had a designer yet, he was told that they were still looking for one. After lunch they returned to the marketing office, and the two men asked Enrique to see my portfolio.

It was close to three in the afternoon when I got the phone call. My brother was so excited he could hardly contain himself. He said I had a job, not at the company where he worked, but at a print shop as an in-house designer. Furthermore, the printer was happy to know this arrangement would only be for one year, which is what my brother and I had decided from the beginning. After one year of working for someone we would then find office space and start our own company.

One year was also the minimum time contract Immigration Canada required to qualify for a visa. Everything seemed to be falling into place in my life, and I was very conscious God was working on my behalf. To me, this was a sign of His blessing, which further made me want to believe that one day I was going to be normal.

Chapter 15: Crossing the Border

On Friday, June 22nd, 1973, I said goodbye to my family in San Jose, and left for Canada in my 1972 Dodge Colt, which was packed with my guitar, my clothes, and as many belongings as I could fit. I was also shipping up my bedroom suite, which included the bed and mattress, nightstand and dresser, stereo, my record collection, and whatever else I had been unable to take with me in the car. These would be coming via a moving company a few days later.

On the first leg of the trip, I made it to just north of Olympia, Washington, where I spent the night in a rest stop. I had sun all the way as I headed north on I-5, and my left arm got quite sunburned from resting on the door. The second day I completed the trip to the Canadian border, where I presented my visa and immigration papers.

I was processed and welcomed into Canada. I called Enrique from the immigration office and told him I had just crossed the border and would meet him at his house. He shared a three bedroom duplex with a friend and they had a bedroom reserved for me.

The rest of the day I spent unloading the car, unpacking the few boxes and suitcases, and getting settled in. I was to start work on the following Monday. There I was at last; I celebrated with Carmen and her husband on Sunday. The drive had really taken it out of me; it was good to just relax.

On Monday I arrived at the printing company and met the man who had hired me a few months earlier. Then I was introduced to the rest of the office staff and the sales team. I was a bit crestfallen when I arrived at the plant because it was an old building, the office furnishings circa 1940. But I kept reminding myself that this arrangement was only for one year and then Enrique and I would join forces, find some office space and do our own thing.

That wasn't all that was a big letdown. My office was not going to be even in that building; it turned out to be a grimy storefront around the corner on a very busy up-hill portion of one of Vancouver's busiest streets. If you stood on the sidewalk in front of the store the traffic noise was almost deafening, especially when trucks and buses strained their engines to make it up the hill, never mind the exhaust fumes and the constant hum of cars going by!

In preparation for my arrival they had moved a couple of old wooden desks into the space and had the phone company install three lines connecting us to the main office and the outside world. I say "us" because the plan was to house one or two of their sales representatives in that storefront along with me. There were no drafting table or art supplies anywhere to be seen.

Fortunately, Enrique had established a relationship with a local graphic arts supplier, and Jack, the owner of the print shop, told me I could go to the store to purchase whatever I needed to do my work. So the first day of work was really spent shopping for all the basic necessities to set up a graphic design office. It wasn't such a bad way to take my mind off the shortcomings, using somebody else's money to get things that I would want for myself.

Call it immaturity or naïveté, but I really believed the doors opening up for me were not simple coincidences; I believed they were God's confirmation for my life, which further bolstered my hope for you-know-what. All these little events were like God's "love notes."

I had not yet given much thought to what church I would be attending. The only church I knew about was the Pentecostal church that had some kind of association with the one near San Jose State. I had actually visited that church on my second visit to Vancouver a year earlier, and had been accosted by one of their members on the way out. Maybe *accosted* is too strong a word. I was confronted and told my long hair, which only came down to just below the collar of my shirt, was not suitable for men, and they had a word of prophecy to this effect. As far as this man was concerned he was relaying God's words of instruction to me; he was serious that I needed to correct my hairstyle as soon as possible. Consequently, his church was not even on the radar for me as a possible church to attend.

The printing company had recently hired two young sales representatives. One was a recent graduate from the British Columbia Institute of Technology's (BCIT) marketing program. I believe the other salesman, Vic, had attended the University of British Columbia (UBC), but I don't recall if he had a degree or not. In any case, the three of us were about the same age and this was less intimidating for me. I soon learned Vic was involved in a tiny church in South Vancouver on a residential street and I thought this was great. Perhaps I would attend church with him one day to check it out. Yet again, I thought this was another *love note* from God.

The dizzying state I found myself in when I first arrived lasted all of that first week in Vancouver. I was trying to orient myself and get used to a different pace of life. I was so used to driving on freeways—and long distances—for just about anything I had to do in California, but city life as I experienced it in Vancouver was definitely different.

I won't talk about the weather, because I could go on and on about the differences. Let's just say I really missed California's climate. Now, however, my perspective on life had this eternal quality to it, and *mere weather* didn't matter as much. I would sing to myself the words of an old Gospel song I learned along the way, "This world is not my home, I'm just a-passing through."

Culturally, British Columbia was so different! I was surprised by how seemingly unfriendly people were the first time I walked downtown by myself. I had gone to purchase a few things I needed at the Hudson's Bay department store, and parked my car a few blocks away. I was accustomed to smiling and acknowledging people as I walk past them, and even saying hello if I met somebody's eye. This is what it was like in California: you said *Hi!* to total strangers and they said *Hi!* back to you. I thought it was strange that now whenever I made eye contact with someone on the sidewalk, or said *Hi!* to them, whether they be male or female, they would immediately look down or turn away.

So startling was this to me, the thought crossed my mind that maybe I was getting this reaction because the fly of my pants might be open. It's true, that's what I thought. As I continued walking I discreetly felt to see if that was the case, but no, that was not it. It seemed so bizarre.

I mentioned this to Enrique when I got home, and he laughed and said, "Welcome to British Columbia," putting the emphasis on the word "*British.*" He said he thought this was the British influence, and to get used to it. But there was something else I found a little strange. Based on my experience working at the restaurant company in California, whenever a new person was added to the team, people would go out of their way to include them socially, especially if they were new in town.

Though I did not really work full-time for the restaurant company, different people had invited me out after work on more than one occasion. I also remembered co-workers often did things together on the weekends—there was a camaraderie among them that was part of the company culture. I sort of expected that to be a universal phenomenon, but at the printing company in Vancouver Friday arrived without any of this kind of mingling taking place. I was surprised because I thought for sure someone might invite me to go out with them or suggest we go somewhere after work, or make plans for the weekend.

I was acutely aware of how, in the past, I had always depended on Enrique's paving the way for me. Things were different now, and this was partly due to the fact I had "religion" and he didn't. This was not lost on him, either. That first week in Vancouver he lay down some ground rules that were very specific: no "proselytizing or evangelizing" him or any of his friends. He said he respected my beliefs and I should respect his, which were not very evident. I don't know why he felt he had to tell me this but I told him he didn't have to worry, that I would keep it to myself.

The living arrangements at the house were a bit uncomfortable for me, since Enrique's roommate had a girlfriend who often spent the night with him. The seismic activity was constant, and I would have been less disturbing if their bedpost didn't thump the wall so loudly when they were in an amorous mood. It was hard not to feel awkward when I saw them the next day.

Though Enrique introduced me to many of his friends it was obvious I had nothing in common with them. They all seemed friendly and easy-going, and I was happy to meet them. Honestly, however, I felt I had more in common with Vic at work than I did with my own brother. It was pretty sobering to realize it was easier to be genuine with Vic, who was a total stranger to me, than it was to be open and honest with Enrique.

My relationship with my older sister, on the other hand, was very different. Carmen and I shared a common bond, thanks to our faith. Though we are eight years apart in age, and she was married and had a young daughter, she went out of her way to make sure I lacked nothing or that I would not be alone on the weekends. She knew Enrique and I no longer had so many things in common with the exception of our interest in graphic design.

After a month, I decided I needed to look for my own place. It was becoming increasingly uncomfortable, not only for me, but for my brother and his friend. I think they must have felt as if a priest had moved into the house with them. Without me saying anything to them about Jesus or the Bible, they were constantly catching themselves swearing in front of me and would hasten to apologize. In fact, they weren't swearing any more than they ever had, it's just they were suddenly more aware of it.

I found a one-bedroom basement suite in the house of an old Austrian couple. It was perfect for me and it was halfway between where Enrique lived and where I worked, so it took less time for me to commute. Work started coming in, slowly at first, and then there was a steady stream of ongoing projects. I was getting paid a straight hourly rate and it didn't matter to the owner, Jack, whether I was working on some stationery or a complete rebranding for one of his customers. I'm convinced he was giving away the graphic design service in order to get the printing jobs, and I felt he was underselling and not taking advantage of some of the opportunities to make the graphic design service a profit center.

For example, logo designs, which most design firms and ad agencies charge big bucks for, were being expensed at my hourly rate, which was substantially lower than what he could have been charging. Like I said earlier, I would just remind myself this was only going to be for a year, and not to let it get under my skin. It certainly reduced the stress level to think of it in those terms.

Vic's little congregation was really a family church in the literal sense. Everybody was related one way or another, and it had been the same size for quite a while. Compared to the growth of some of the churches I attended in California, which were growing like crazy— as evidenced by the number of weekly baptisms—this little chapel's growth seemed stunted. As a result, I was fairly noncommittal and did not feel obliged to remain there. I started looking for something closer to what I had experienced in California.

While I had been involved with a Catholic parish in San Jose, I didn't really see myself as a Catholic, and felt quite free to attend any church, regardless of denomination. Among the churches I often visited in California were Peninsula Bible Church (PBC), in Palo Alto, and Los Gatos Christian. These were large churches and attracted a lot of younger people, both high school and college-age.

In the West End of Vancouver, which is one of the most densely populated neighborhoods in North America, and within walking distance of the downtown core, I discovered an interesting Christian coffee house called the *Hobbit House*. My sister lived in the West End, and I would go and spend a lot of time with her on the weekends, returning to my basement suite around 10:30 or 11 p.m. I always drove past the Hobbit House on my way home and wondered what it was all about.

Curiosity got the better of me one night, so I pulled over and walked in just as it was closing for the night. There was a guy about my age who was sweeping the floor and putting chairs upside down on top of the tables. He invited me to come back the following weekend. I told him I was new in town and I was curious as to what the Hobbit House was all about. He told me a little bit about what went on, and then asked where I was from. When I said that I was from San Jose, California, he got all excited and introduced himself. He told me he was from California, too, and had graduated from Stanford University, which is not far from San Jose. His name was Peter, and his wife, Corrine, were both graduate students at the University of British Columbia and worked part-time for First Baptist Church, which actually ran Hobbit House. As caretakers and directors of the coffee house, Peter and Corrine lived upstairs; they became my closest friends in Vancouver.

Since I played guitar and sang, I was soon one of the many people who provided entertainment at the Hobbit House on weekends. I have mentioned distractions were always a good thing for me. They allowed me to focus on things I enjoyed, or had some talent and ability for; and, in a sense, helped numb the gender thing. Again, I saw all of this as another love note from God.

Now, after having lived here for most of my life, I can sincerely say these initial impressions I had about people in Vancouver were very skewed and superficial. Contrary to my initial reaction, I have found the people in Vancouver every bit as friendly as the people in California. Admittedly, when I came to Canada, I was still very immature and superficial, and saw things through a very narrow lens.

Chapter 16: Homesickness or Love?

I had been in Vancouver for about two months by now, and had been sending Rachel postcards with short updates about once a week. She would reply in kind a few days later, and we went back and forth like this through the rest of summer. In the process I was coming to realize something I had not allowed myself to see when I was living in San Jose. As I mentioned, I had found Vancouver to be a difficult place to get to know people. If it hadn't been for Peter and Corinne, my brother Enrique, and my sister Carmen and her husband, I think I would have been lost.

I missed the close contact I had with friends in California, but soon recognized that I especially missed my friendship with Rachel. I had a problem—I had no idea how she felt about me since we had never talked about this kind of stuff. Though her postcards to me were friendly and cheerful, I didn't know if she was just being kind to me, or if there was more to it than that.

Superimposed on this was my interpretation of what God might be doing; I wondered if His plan for me was to be a husband and through this I would experience the healing I wanted so desperately. The more I thought about it, the more it made sense to me. And thoughts about Rachel and her amazing qualities, not just as a Christian but as a woman, made me want to be the best husband I could possibly be for her. I agonized about how I would be able to find out for sure, one way or another, if she was interested in me in that way. I had never done this before, and had never felt this way, either. I was ill-prepared and didn't know how to even bring up the subject with her. A postcard would definitely not have been the way. A phone call, I concluded, would have also been impossible for me, because I would not have been able to get the words out in a way that would have conveyed my sincere love.

I felt safe bringing the subject up with Peter and Corinne, and asked them for advice. They asked me a lot of questions, because up to now, they knew nothing about Rachel; I had never said anything to anyone about her. How did we meet? What did she do for a living? Did I know her family? Corinne suggested I write her a letter to convey everything I just said to them. For all I knew, it could be a one-way street. I needed to know if she had similar feelings for me as I had for her. It seemed simple enough.

I went home that night and poured my heart out on paper. I felt obliged to apologize over and over again and to say I wasn't trying to put her on the spot. I needed her to tell me if she cared for me. "Yes" or "No"–I would understand. I don't know how many times I started the letter over. I was having a very difficult time conveying things in a way she would appreciate, and didn't want her to think I was simply homesick.

I met with Peter and Corinne that weekend and showed them a draft of the letter. Corinne suggested a couple of minor changes, but felt the letter was very sincere and from the heart, and that any woman receiving it would think the same.

That week I sent the letter instead of the usual postcard. I figured it would be in her hands by the following Tuesday or Wednesday. I had no idea if, when or how she would reply. Would she write back, would she call, or would she ignore me?

I was sick with anticipation for the next few days. Time just did not move fast enough that week! By the following Friday I still had not heard from her, and I was going crazy. I gave her the benefit of the doubt in case the letter had not gone by air but was in a truck somewhere. Believe it or not, after four weeks of waiting I still had not heard from her and didn't know what to do. Should I call her or should I send another postcard? But what if she got the letter and read it and was horrified at the things I had said? Maybe, I concluded, she didn't like me and/or did not share the same feelings for me.

My self-image in front of Peter and Corinne took a dive, and I was almost reluctant to see them. Since they were in on this scheme, they kept asking me every time they saw me if I heard from Rachel.

It wasn't supposed to work like this. I was climbing walls and, with my heart in my throat, would arrive home and open the door to my basement suite, turning on the entrance light to see what mail had been put through the mail slot earlier that day. But I never saw a letter or postcard from Rachel.

One Sunday after church I purchased a postcard and wrote a very terse message to her. It said something to the effect that I thought she was more mature than this, and that if I had said anything in the letter that made her feel uncomfortable, she should have said so, and I would have understood. I continued that I still wanted to hear from her one way or another, and to please write. I put a stamp on it and dropped it into a mailbox. It was the Sunday before American Thanksgiving, a detail I had forgotten since the Canadian version of that holiday is celebrated in the second week of October.

The following Wednesday I attended a Bible study at a church I had found in my neighborhood with a large college and career group. I got home about ten o'clock at night, and just as I was unlocking the front door, my phone started ringing. I was able to answer it just in time before the caller hung up. It was Rachel. I was taken by surprise and muttered something unintelligible.

She asked, "Is this Jim?"

"Yes." My heart was racing.

Then she said, "Happy Thanksgiving!"

"Oh yeah, it's Thanksgiving tomorrow in the States—I had forgotten—Happy Thanksgiving to you!" I blurted out.

Quietly, almost inaudibly, she said she had received my latest postcard and was a little confused. She had gone through all our correspondence and wasn't sure what I was talking about in the post card. I responded by telling her how I had been climbing the walls for the last month and a half waiting for her to write me.

"I've been climbing walls too," she replied.

I couldn't believe what she had just said. I asked, "You have?"

"Yes," she answered.

I then told her I had come to realize how important she was to me, how I thought about her all the time and that I loved her.

Rachel answered, "I love you too!"

"You do?"

"Yes!" She admitted, "I love you and I thought you had stopped writing because you had met someone else." Our breakdown in communication resulted from her never receiving my four-page letter. It was lost in the mail somewhere between Vancouver and San Jose, so when she got my tersely worded postcard, it made no sense to her.

I know I should have that first conversation memorized, but that is all I can remember about the phone call. We agreed to call each other once a week and would begin to explore what the next steps should be if we got together. That was the plan.

Unable to wait a whole week before talking to her again, I called her the next day. We started calling each other on a daily basis. I couldn't get enough of her! Our long-distance phone bills that first month would have paid for one of us to fly back and forth twice.

My parents celebrated that Thanksgiving in San Jose with only Angela and John, the two children remaining at home. I'm not sure whose idea it was, Carmen's maybe, but the next thing I knew our parents, with Angela and John, were coming up to Vancouver to celebrate Christmas. Previously, ever since Carmen and Enrique had moved up to Vancouver, they had returned to California for the Christmas holiday. This would be the first Christmas, in the fourteen years since we left Colombia, that was going to be celebrated somewhere else besides San Jose.

Peter and Corinne were going down to California to celebrate Christmas with their families, and had asked me if I would like to stay at the Hobbit House during the two weeks they would be away. They were the same two weeks my parents would be coming up to Vancouver. This gave me the idea to find out if Rachel could get time off so she, too, could join us all for our first Christmas in Canada.

Once again, things were falling into place; yet another love note from God, I thought. Then I found out my brother-in-law's younger brother and his wife, who only lived about a block away from the Hobbit House, would be going to Toronto to celebrate Christmas with her family, and that their apartment would be vacant. Carmen inquired on our behalf, and they were more than happy to let Rachel stay in the apartment. This was perfect, because we would not be put on the spot to decide if she should stay in the same place with me. We were both very sincere and cognizant of our Christian views on marriage, and it would have violated our sense of what was right and wrong if we had shared a bed.

With all these details worked out, I called Rachel to suggest this crazy idea of her coming to Vancouver for Christmas. I asked her, first, if she was going to be taking any time off over the holidays. She said their office was going to be closed for two weeks because the doctor was taking his family on a ski vacation to Lake Tahoe. I couldn't believe my ears! I asked her if I sent her an airplane ticket would she like to come up for Christmas, and then shared with her that my parents were coming up with Angela and John. (I had introduced her to my family when I still lived in San Jose.) She answered *Yes!* she would love to come up to Vancouver. Her alternative was to stay home in San Jose, since she had decided not to go to Texas that year.

Peter and Corinne's departure overlapped Rachel's arrival by a couple of days. Since Peter sang in the choir, he invited us to First Baptist Church's presentation of *The Messiah*. After the performance there was a party for the choir at a house overlooking Vancouver in an area known as the British Properties. Rachel and I were a little nervous about crashing this party, which was for church members only, but Peter insisted it would be okay.

What an amazing house! It belonged to one of the wealthiest families in Vancouver, members of the church. With floor-to-ceiling picture windows and a panoramic view, on a clear day, one could see Vancouver Island to the west, the coastal mountains to the east, and as far south as the entrance to Puget Sound and the mountains of the Olympic Peninsula on the horizon.

Peter knew everyone, and wanted us to meet some of the people who were there. The first time he introduced us, he said, "I would like you to meet Jim and his fiancée, Rachel." I saw the look of shock on Rachel's face as we both gasped. We had not even discussed the engagement yet. Not wanting to embarrass Peter, we said nothing to him but gave each other this funny look.

She pulled me aside and she asked me nervously, "Did you tell Peter that we were engaged?"

"No!" I stammered, "But how do you like the sound of it?"

She smiled, "I like it a lot!"

I grinned, "I do, too!"

And that was how we got engaged. Not the way I had ever expected it to happen; we had never dated officially, yet here we were engaged and it seemed so right. I was so grateful to God because I was going to be normal at last. He had answered my prayer.

Chapter 17: The Countdown

You know the saying, "That was a Christmas to remember?" I guess you could say Christmas 1973 was for us one to remember. Unfortunately, I don't remember much about it—it was a complete blur to me. There was so much to take in and so little time for it all. It was a milestone to be sure: the first family Christmas in Canada; the twenty-third Christmas since we left Colombia; Rachel and I engaged; and my parents warming up to the idea that they, too, might move to Canada.

Rachel and I had our first official date in Vancouver as well. We laughed at the fact we were engaged before our first "romantic" date. We had certainly done things in reverse. It didn't take long for Rachel and me to start thinking about a wedding day. She would be returning to California, which meant we would have to endure a long-distance romance for several months. We ruled out spring and summer since it would have been too soon for Rachel to do all the necessary things to relocate to Canada.

As we looked at the calendar we were cognizant of the fact that whatever date we picked should be close to another important *family* date so those who had to travel could kill two birds with one stone. We didn't want to do it near Easter, Thanksgiving or Christmas—and we wanted it to be on a Saturday. Since my mom's birthday is three days before my parents' anniversary in October, this seemed like the most convenient time of the year, and a fall wedding was also appealing to us. That year Mom's birthday was on a Saturday, and we concluded that this would be a wonderful way to commemorate her birthday. So that's the day we chose—totally oblivious to the fact it was also her fiftieth birthday that year.

It was hard saying goodbye to Rachel at the airport, but we were in love. The only thing that made it bearable for me was the knowledge that in just a few months we would be together forever. I was going to beat my demon, and was resolved more than ever to present myself to her on our wedding day as a transformed person, free from the curse of my gender confusion. I found strength to focus on my love for her and our future together.

In the meantime, she was busy planning with her friends. Our wedding would be simple and unpretentious and the reception would be a potluck in the church hall—organized by her friends. Since we were trying to save money for the start of our life together—including her move up to Canada—we had agreed to keep the phone calls to a minimum to avoid the large bill we had incurred in the fall.

Since the wedding was going to be in San Jose, it meant I would need to go have the blood test done for the marriage license and finalize the arrangements with the minister. This also included several joint sessions with him, one of his prerequisites if he was to perform the wedding ceremony.

I would need to be in San Jose for a couple of weeks to accomplish all of this, but first I wanted to be free of my commitment to the printing company. My contract with them was ending in June, and I would need a few days, possibly a few weeks, to find office space with Enrique. We had already incorporated the company and opened a bank account where we were depositing money to build up a small cash reserve. Enrique, being the business part of the equation, had gotten to know our bank manager on a first name basis.

I don't know how he did it, but the banker approved a company loan so Enrique and I could buy two identical, brand-new 1974 VW vans seven-seater vans. I didn't need much convincing, since by removing the seats, Rachel and I would be able to drive up after our wedding with all her belongings. I took delivery of the van and a few weeks later; in mid-August I drove down to California.

Rachel and I had not spent so many days together in a row since the two weeks at Christmas time. She lived in a little one-bedroom cottage behind a house in Santa Clara. She had only lived there a few months and was sad to leave such a cute little place behind. Before I returned to Vancouver, she wanted to make me a special dinner. I arrived and she had set her tiny table with candles and flowers, and had made the place look amazing. For dinner, we had roasted Cornish game hens and served them with brown rice and salad. It was all so lovely. So Rachel.

After we finished dinner and cleaned up we moved to the couch and were listening to some soft music. As we talked about things the phone rang. Rachel answered, and, after a brief exchange with the caller, her body language changed completely as she leaned away from me as if to prevent me from overhearing the conversation. She answered the mysterious caller, no, she had not seen "him" for a while, and the last time she had seen "him," he had told her he was thinking of maybe becoming a hairdresser in a kidding sort of way. Then she added she had not spoken to "him" since.

She was visibly shaken and uncomfortable as she hung up the phone. I asked her who had called and what the call was all about—it was all too strange. She told me it was Stewart, the man who led the Bible study at the Catholic Church who had also recruited her to be one of the people to come to the high school retreat. She explained that before moving to the cottage, when she had lived with Stewart's younger sister in another house, this fellow, Mark, who had been part of the Wallace's Bible study group, had offered to come by once a week to mow their lawn as a favor. They gladly accepted his Christian charity.

Rachel continued that one Saturday, when she was home alone, Mark came by to discuss something with them. Rachel explained that Susan was at work, but he asked if he could use the washroom. When he came out, he was wearing some of Susan's clothing—taken from the laundry hamper—and had applied makeup to his face.

"This is what I wanted to talk to you about; I came to confess this is what I've been doing when I come to mow the lawn."

Rachel and Susan had given Mark the key to the house so he could go into the garage to get the lawnmower. He admitted to Rachel he had tried on some of her things but they were too small for him and he had been wearing Susan's clothing only since they were a better fit. Rachel told him that was something he was going to have to discuss with Susan; she told him to go back into the bathroom, take the makeup and clothing off and leave immediately. Rachel was very visibly upset as she shared this with me.

The reason Stewart called was to find out if she knew whether Mark had modified his behavior, or if he had made further contact. Mark was now applying for some church-related position and had confessed his misdeeds to absolve himself.

As Rachel was talking about this incident, I was terrified and was faced with a monumental choice. Should I tell her about me and risk everything, or should I keep my mouth shut? The disgust in Rachel's voice sent shudders through me—she would not want to marry me if she really knew my secret. Why was this happening? Was God testing me? I couldn't think straight. Was my life going to crash into a pile of ashes?

As I debated with myself what I should do, I prayed to God to help me. I was desperate. I wanted to believe His promise, that all my sins had been forgiven and had been cast into the depths of the sea.

After a moment of awkward silence I opened my mouth, and began by admitting to Rachel that I had put on my sister's clothing to see what it felt like. I told her I suspected most guys had probably done the same thing out of curiosity. Rachel conceded stuff like that happened, but this was different. I was sick to my stomach as fear gripped me—but this was all the courage I could muster up; it was all I could think to tell her. I couldn't bring myself to make a total disclosure, and I argued with myself that, if God had already forgiven me, then I no longer needed to bring up my past. I then did something I had become very adept at doing—I changed the subject as if to say it was not a big deal, just a normal thing for boys to do.

I wish I could say my conscience has not bothered me about this. How would Rachel have really responded if I had confessed everything to her? I don't know. At the time, I still did not know I was transgender. I knew more what I was *not* than what I was. I did know that I wanted to be Rachel's husband more than anything in the world. I wanted to be the best husband I could be for her.

Chapter 18: I Promise

Back in Vancouver it was time to get serious about work. My brother and I found an office in the historic part of the city, known as Gastown, which was enjoying a renaissance of sorts. Heritage buildings were being transformed into retail and office space, and the main street itself was being repaved with red bricks. Our office was in a funky triangular brick building that sat at the point of the triangular block. It housed a nightclub in the basement, some small shops on the main floor, and offices on the second and third floors. Ours was on the second floor at the point of the building. Almost all the other tenants in the building were creative types, so it was a great place for networking as well as camaraderie and friendship.

Little by little we started to get work, but then we got a lucky break thanks to the work I had been doing for the group of restaurants in California. We were introduced to the marketing director of a relatively new restaurant company known as the Keg 'n Cleaver—a steak and lobster concept with a trademark all-you-can-eat salad bar. Thanks to this client, we were able to get established, and the company became our much-needed bread-and-butter account.

Many of the freelance graphic designers around us were primarily working for various advertising agencies on a contract basis. There seemed to be no end to the amount of that work available, so we, too, began to introduce ourselves and to show our portfolio. However, being new at the game we didn't realize that we were shooting ourselves in the feet when we answered what kind of work we were interested in.

The people we would typically be seeing at the agencies were art directors, and when we would answer that we wanted to art direct and design, we didn't realize this was a declaration that we were going to step on their turf. Ad agencies are very territorial and protective. Basically, when an agency hires a designer, it is to reproduce and/or execute *their* ideas; they want your skilled hands, not your creative brains. Here we were offering both. It was just as well because the few jobs we got from the ad agencies were really not very much fun to work on for two reasons: 1) some art directors were nit-picky prima donnas, 2) we were reduced to being robots and production artist.

Our business plan was a work in progress. In the end, we developed a strategy that we would go for a niche market and serve small clients who needed agency quality work, but who would be too small to engage an agency and could not afford agency rates.

I found a new basement suite that was brighter and a bit larger than the first one; this would be Rachel's and my new home. Thanks to the intensity of starting a new business and setting up the apartment, September flew by, and before I knew it, it was time to head down to California for the wedding. I had never felt so assured in my male identity as I did then. God seemed to be working, and I was sure I would soon be completely fixed. I didn't want to do anything that would jinx that process.

With all these wonderful things happening around me, and sensing I was enjoying blessing upon blessing, I was oblivious at first—but then I realized my brother Enrique was not doing so great. It was hard for him to admit, but his personal life was unraveling. He had always been the strong one, the one I would look up to and get direction from, but now the roles were reversed, and he was coming to me for guidance. He had many questions having to do with spiritual issues.

I remember soon after he gave me the ultimatum that he didn't want me talking to him and his housemate about religion, I had prayed to God to help Enrique see his need. I asked God to do whatever it would take to get his attention, even if it meant something tragic happening to me. I was willing to suffer for Enrique if that is what it would take for him to get serious about God.

I think God answered that prayer, because in a series of events his heart was broken by the woman he had fallen in love with. He was inconsolable. He called me one night in tears because she had decided she could not marry him, and he could not understand why and wondered how this could be happening. Shortly after this he finally came to the point where he, too, surrendered his life to God in a new way, and we grew closer than we had ever been before. I was no longer his "little brother," but an equal. Everything was going to be new; everything was going to be different.

For me, marrying Rachel was to mark the beginning of a new life with hope for the future, free of the guilt and confusion I had lived with all my life.

The wedding was everything I hoped it would be. Rachel was beautiful, and I was so proud to declare my love for her in front of family and friends, while at the same time I was so humbled by the fact she loved me.

For our honeymoon trip we drove up to Vancouver in the van, loaded with Rachel's things, but we spent our wedding night in a cabin in Ben Lomond in the Santa Cruz Mountains. Our mutual timidity and bashfulness gradually melted away as we embraced for the first time. Her love, meekness and gentleness that night will be forever emblazoned in my memory as the best gift I have ever received. Her love caused me to forget about all my fears and apprehensions; and my insecurity as a man finally seemed like it could be a thing of the past.

That night I was so grateful to God and believed he was answering my prayers. And Rachel's love for me made we want to believe this all the more; I wanted it to be true for her too.

Sunday morning we drove to Santa Cruz and had breakfast and I'll never forget how wonderful it felt to be sitting across from her at the table holding her hands and just gazing into her eyes. I was so grateful to God and hoped this was the beginning of a new me.

After breakfast, we drove back to San Jose to load up the van and say our goodbyes to family and her friends. Then we headed north to San Francisco and across the Golden Gate Bridge. We had booked a motel room in a cozy lodge in Russian River, where we spent Sunday night. We then continued up the coast on U.S. Highway 1, all the way to the mouth of the Columbia River, before turning east to connect with I-5 to head north. It was typical autumn weather, sunny with a bit of chill in the air and the trees starting to change color. I felt as if we were on a *Magical Mystery Tour*. It was all good. It was all very good!

When we got to the Canadian border it started to sprinkle. This was the first bit of precipitation we had experienced on our trip and, as Rachel points out today, it rained nonstop for a month. She wondered what it was she had gotten herself into. She went through withdrawal for California weather.

Though she had been working for several years in an oral surgeon's office she wasn't sure if that's what she wanted to do again. I had met one of the couples from First Baptist Church who volunteered at the Hobbit House on the weekends. His family owned a food and restaurant supply company and offered Rachel a job on telephone sales. This was all before computers, when orders were typed onto four-part *NCR* forms as the orders were placed by telephone. Rachel had good typing skills, so she accepted the job.

The great thing was that this company was just three blocks away at the other end of Gastown. We could drive to work together. More importantly, we were able to meet for lunch every day.

We started going to the church with the college and career group where I had been attending some Bible studies; but we also got involved assisting the youth pastor with the high school students. They welcomed us as a couple, and for the next few months we helped out once a week with the group's activities.

My older sister Carmen and her husband had their second child that January. I have to admit being around her little baby boy got us thinking seriously about starting our own family. We had made some decisions and set some goals for ourselves, determining, if and when our children came, that Rachel would be a stay-at-home mom. We also decided we would try to stay in one place to give our children the chance to grow up and to develop roots in one spot—unlike the two of us, who had moved several times throughout our childhoods.

By this time, my parents had decided to sell their business and their home in California and to move to Canada. Dad came to Vancouver to scout out job prospects and left mom to pack their belongings. He found a job managing a dry cleaners in Vancouver, and got the right of first refusal in the event the owner chose to sell the business. It was a good arrangement and made it possible for my parents to immigrate before the summer.

The only unhappy people were my younger brother and sister, who felt as if they were being pulled away from their friends without much say in the matter. John had one year left in high school, and Angela was working as a dental assistant in San Jose, but I'm sure our mom would not have wanted her to stay in California by herself.

By March of 1975, the whole family was reunited again, and permanently, from Colombia to British Columbia by way of California. It had taken 15 years.

Chapter 19: Starting a Family

Our doctor's office called me at work about ten in the morning with the pregnancy test results. We were going to have a baby, and I got the news first because Rachel had told our doctor to call me with results, since she would be unable to take the call at work. I called Rachel to tell her I wanted to see her during her coffee break, and left immediately.

On the way I stopped at a gift shop and bought a little porcelain Beatrix Potter rabbit that was tucked into in a cozy straw bed with a baby blue blanket. They wrapped it in tissue and put it in its box and tied a ribbon around it. I presented it to her, and when she opened it we both began to cry with joy.

How much more proof did I need, I thought to myself, that I was a man? The deep joy of seeing Rachel aglow with happiness, and the knowledge we had a baby of our own on the way, was beyond words. Why, then, was I being tormented with contrary feelings about myself, especially at this time? It was a spiritual attack, I told myself. "Satan always wants to sabotage, and attack and destroy."

I was too deep into my obligations, not just to Rachel but also to myself, and so could not risk saying anything to anyone. None of this made sense to me. I had really hoped marriage and fatherhood would have dispelled all of these feelings and thoughts.

Despite my best efforts to train my mind and not dwell on my confusion it was impossible to avoid these thoughts. The reminders were everywhere I looked. The only way I was able to bear this "assault" was by spiritualizing the whole thing, and labeling it as Satan's ploy to tempt me. This was going to be my cross to bear, and it was starting to look like it would never leave me.

Adding to my determination and desire to be the best husband I could be for Rachel was the imperative to also be the best father I could be for our baby. The pressure I was under to be "pure" was beyond words. If I could have flogged it out of me, I would have.

Without cataloging all the scriptures I used in my valiant yet vain attempt at shoring up my resolve, let me just say one thing: I beat myself up with them. I was unhappy with my apparent failure to claim God's promises to defeat the enemy. To say I felt defeated is an understatement.

My knowledge of scripture and my ability to articulate my faith when called upon became my cover-up. Our church friends considered me so "mature" and "spiritual," but I felt like one of the hypocrites Jesus accused of being whitewashed tombs full of dead men's bones.

With a baby on the way it was time for us to find a more suitable house for our young family. Our basement suite was in East Vancouver, and we wanted to live more centrally, closer to my first basement suite, which I found so convenient. We found a two-bedroom house for rent; it was perfect. The owner was a man from Hungary who lived downstairs in the basement. He worked for two or three weeks at a time in lumber and pulp mills as a pipe fitter with the Boilermakers' Union. He would come home for a few days and then go up north to another job. He loved gardening and maintained the beautifully manicured backyard that was ours to use whenever we wanted.

We were so happy, and life had all the appearances of normalcy—and that is how I wanted it for Rachel. Whenever the thought crossed my mind that I needed to share my secret struggles with her, I would be reminded of the look of disgust on her face when she was telling me about Mark, the cross-dresser. How could I tell her now? It would crush her and rob her joy and anticipation for the baby inside her. No, it was too late for that. I was going to have to keep this to myself and never, ever, open my mouth.

I don't know how I managed to survive, I was so schizophrenic. In the movie *A Beautiful Mind* there is a scene where we look into a room that has all the walls completely covered with notes, magazine, and newspaper clippings. That scene aptly portrays what it was like in my head. I labeled and categorized this identity-thing to death. I had to keep it in the realm of good versus evil and make everything black and white. Rules upon rules, disciplines upon disciplines. It was exhausting.

Rachel was due any day, and we had invited some friends over for dinner. But before we could sit down to enjoy the meal Rachel's water broke. We were all delirious with excitement and our friends wished us well and said goodbye as we left for the hospital. Her contractions had not yet started when we got to the hospital, so the nurses prepped her and we waited. We had attended a prenatal class together, so I got to be in the delivery room when our son was born just after sunrise. I was so grateful when I saw he was healthy and he had ten fingers and ten toes! I had this nagging fear that God was going to punish me for my "perverted mind" and our baby would not be perfect—how could I expect anything else? I apologized to God asking for His forgiveness for my lack of faith, and for allowing my mind to have such morbid thoughts.

My parents and sisters came to the hospital as soon as I called them with the news and, for a brief moment, I experienced a profound sense of wholeness. I wanted that sense of peace to last forever.

The first time I had slept alone since we got married was the night after our son was born. I am sorry to say it is also the first time I finally caved in. I was in the bathroom getting ready for bed and hanging on the back of the door was one of Rachel's flannel nightgowns. I put my nose to smell her scent, then pressed my face against it with my eyes closed as I thought of her, and how beautiful and happy she looked holding our son to her breast. I took the nightgown off the hook and brought it into the bedroom, as if it was a safety blanket—and up to this point everything would have been okay.

I don't know what compelled me to slip it over my head, put my arms through the sleeves and then lay down in bed. My mind raced as I tried to go to sleep; I felt a terrible guilt. What would Rachel say and do if she knew? I think I knew what the answer to that was, but she *wasn't* there and no one was ever going to know. I finally managed to fall a sleep and spent the whole night in her nightgown.

To say I was remorseful the following morning is another understatement. I felt horrible and I asked God for forgiveness and cleansing. I wondered, too, why I had given in after having been so *good* for so long. How ironic and how wrong, I thought, that in less than twenty-four hours after the child I fathered had been born I was back to where I had been before—unable to make sense of my life—feeling shame and resorting again to the need for secrecy.

But now, too, there was a new focus in my life. It is amazing how quickly your priorities change when there is a new little person in your life. One minute you're free to be spontaneous, and the next you are no longer a free agent; it is as if your wings get clipped. Every couple I know has gone through this readjustment of schedules as their life suddenly revolves around the needs of their baby. The mysterious thing is, though life gets turned upside down, you can't imagine having it any other way. The joy felt and the love that suddenly springs from the heart for the child is like nothing ever experienced before. This was certainly true in our case.

I'm sure it's a universal thing for parents to pray their children will not be afflicted with their problems and issues. We ask God to spare them the suffering we have experienced, and wish for our children a life free of adversity and sorrow.

As a Christian I believed, and still do, that we live in a broken world, and are a wounded people. Though we live in a world that is broken, wounded and fallen, God sent someone from outside this world to rescue us, a Savior—Jesus. This is what gave me hope as I prayed for our son to be spared from my "affliction."

For the first few months after our son was born I was a defeated person spiritually. I could not reconcile myself to my internal struggle. Even though I had fathered a child, I still questioned my gender identity. During this time, we had stopped going to church, and no longer had any obligations or responsibilities with the high school group. Since we had been involved as a couple, I did not want to continue without Rachel. This was the convenient excuse I used to isolate myself spiritually.

Our friends Peter and Corinne had also made some changes, and were no longer working with First Baptist Church. They were now attending a new church that met primarily in homes, called "households," and all the households had a joint celebration on Sundays in a rented community center. What was novel about this church was how the real focus for the life of the congregation was these small groups. There were no paid ministers or staff. The leadership consisted of lay people with regular jobs; they formed a Deacons' Board. Peter and Corinne invited us to come to one of the Sunday evening joint celebrations, where we fell in love with the concept and with the people. The church was called Dayspring Fellowship.

We transitioned very easily into the life of this church, and, because Peter and I had a history of making music together, I was soon involved in aspects of the worship during the Sunday celebrations. The format of the weekly household meetings made it easy to come with the baby, and for Rachel to take part, since the little ones were watched by the older children while the adults did "church."

It was a safe and nurturing environment for all, and quite different from all the traditional churches we had attended. On Sundays things were a little different and the service resembled a more traditional Protestant format. The children who came were taken to another room and usually babysat by the parents with babies, since it was much easier for the moms this way.

With help from my parents, we were able to purchase a small eight hundred square-foot fixer-upper house with two bedrooms, one bath, and a low-ceiling unfinished basement where we could set up the washer and dryer. The idea was we would gut the interior, insulate it, refinish all the surfaces, and install double glazed windows.

We took possession of the house in September, 1977, and then Rachel went to Texas for a month with our son while the renovations were taking place. I was able to have it ready in time for their return.

From all indications life was good. No, it was great! My love for Rachel grew each day, as did my love for our son. I rededicated all of my efforts to maintaining a "pure" perspective on my life. How could I possibly risk harming these two people who meant more to me than anything in the world?

Tenaciously, I adopted an even more harsh set of rules for myself, hating my tendency to feel inadequate as a man. I don't know where it came from, but I had an inordinate fear of something terrible happening to our son as punishment for my "sinfulness." Our little boy used to stand at the front window and blow kisses to me as I would drive off to work. I was often reduced to tears as I pulled away, pleading with God to please protect him and not let anything harm him.

A year after moving into our house we found out we were pregnant again. Our second son was born in the summer of 1979. We were able to accommodate both boys in their small bedroom by purchasing a bunk bed. We were so blessed to have two healthy boys and our joy knew no bounds.

With the birth of our second son the tension in my life was reaching a breaking point. All my efforts to suppress and deny my problem had not worked as I had hoped, and I no longer expected that God was going to fix this. If, after getting married and having two sons, I still had this confusion about my gender, then how was I going to survive?

Chapter 20: Full of Beans & Fessing Up

One legacy of our family's life in California was our new liking to Mexican food. It was very different from Colombian food, even though we had dishes with the same Spanish names. It's not that we ate Mexican food all the time but, when we did, we really enjoyed it. One of Mom's alterations customers, Josefina, owned three very popular Mexican restaurants with her husband. As Josefina and Mom became good friends, we feasted several times at *El Gordo,* their flagship location in Los Gatos, California.

Before my parents moved up to Canada those of us who were already in Vancouver would often reminisce about the great meals we had in Josefina's restaurant. Unfortunately, Mexican food was not readily available in Vancouver. We craved the food so much we even made junkets across the border to Washington State so we could buy tortillas and other Mexican ingredients to make the food for ourselves. We called these *tortilla runs.*

At one point we even convinced mom to tell Josefina they should consider opening a restaurant in Vancouver. "Well, Vancouver is so far away and we have our hands full here; with these three restaurants it would be an impossibility. But you know what? Your family should open a restaurant and I will give you all the recipes." That was her promise, and when Mom told us what Josefina had said we could hardly believe our ears! This now became our family's little fantasy.

After my parents moved to Vancouver, the arrangement my Dad had made with the owner of the dry-cleaner fizzled, but my father was not deterred. He found another dry-cleaning plant for sale, and the owner was willing to help finance the purchase. Mom and

Dad were now operating their own business in Vancouver in an excellent location not far from where we lived. They were also fortunate to find a house in the neighborhood, the design and architecture of which reminded them of the building style at the country club in Bogotá. They felt at home.

I have to stop right here just to say how much I admire my Father for having the stamina and wherewithal at his age (he was fifty-seven) to start life yet again, in a different country. The one concern that nagged him was getting older and approaching the traditional retirement age of sixty-five in just a few years. He also realized everything he had was dependent on their business investment.

Dad worried about what would happen if he got ill or, worse yet, died. Then who would take care of the business, and what would happen to Mom? He knew none of us were even remotely interested in taking over the dry-cleaning business or helping him run it. He feared we would have to sell the business in a "fire sale," and would not realize its true value.

Dad called our bluff one day when were fantasizing about opening a Mexican restaurant. He told us about his concern with the dry cleaners, and said he was prepared to sell it and put the money towards a restaurant as long as we all promised to help run it; the whole family would have to be involved. It was a preposterous idea, but he had an ace up his sleeve. One of his dry-cleaning customers owned a Spanish restaurant in the West side area of Vancouver known as Kitsilano. This man was having the same concern about the restaurant that Dad was having about the dry cleaners. His children did not want to be part of it, so he was looking for a buyer.

One day the man came in to the cleaners and Dad asked him if he had sold the restaurant. He had. But the new owners had run it into the ground in a very short time and were now desperate to unload it. He suggested that if we were serious about buying the restaurant we should contact them and make them an offer.

Talk about a turn of events! Dad's idea was for us to purchase the restaurant at a salvage price and transform it into a Mexican restaurant. This would take little effort since the Spanish decor was ideal. We discussed this crazy idea and decided if we were, in fact, going to be the recipients of Josefina's recipes, we might have a chance. To make a long story short, this is exactly what our family did. We opened Las Margaritas, a California-style Mexican restaurant in Vancouver in September of 1980.

Since I had worked in a restaurant kitchen when I lived in California I was designated by the family to go down to San Jose for two weeks to be tutored by Josefina's husband at one of their restaurants. It was so hilarious! Joseafina's husband said to me, "We don't have anything written down; it's all in the head. You are just going to have to watch and take notes."

And that is what I did. Their cooks just opened this and that and scooped, poured and added ingredients by eye. I would try to ascertain the quantities by volume or weight, and took copious notes that I had to re-write along with the procedures. I had a blast—and the best part was that when we tested the recipes in Vancouver, they all worked!

Enrique knew a Mexican girl whose dad was a chef in Los Angeles. We convinced him to come up to Vancouver to help us set up the kitchen. His visa was approved quickly because we were able to demonstrate to Immigration Canadian there were no Mexican chefs in Canada with his skill. That was another lucky break.

While I was in California the rest of the family was busy cleaning and painting the restaurant. We were closed for two months while we got all our ducks in a row. Enrique and I got busy contacting our clients to tell them we were cutting back on hours for a new venture. It was a little strange to be doing that, but we had agreed to dive into the restaurant business with both feet.

At about this time I came to the conclusion the reason God did not answer my prayer was because I had not been forthright and honest with my wife. I had squandered the opportunity to disclose to her and to be truthful about me before we got married, and I could not change that now. But if we were, as I believed, joined and as one before God, then I had an obligation to be completely transparent and honest with her—I shuddered at the thought. However, I could see no other way for me to expect God to honor my prayers for healing than by disclosing to Rachel the full extent of my brokenness.

I wrote a letter as a confession and shared with her the best I could about my problem, my feelings of inadequacy as a man, the sense of disconnection with my body and how much I feared she would not want me as a result. I asked for forgiveness for not having been completely honest with her that night in San Jose. The only way I could explain my behavior was by claiming I too had a fascination with women's clothing. That was the only way I could explain it.

Cross-dressing, or the need to feel feminine, was the symptom, but not the cause. I didn't understand what made me feel the way I did; I certainly didn't know it was a medical condition. I interpreted it simply as my sinful nature.

I agonized about how I would put all these things, the words I would use, and how I was going to present it to her. I decided the best and only thing I could do was read it to her in person. One night after the boys were asleep I finally worked up the courage to tell her that I had something I needed to discuss with her. We sat on the couch and I read her the letter. It was all so intense; I could not keep myself from choking up. I composed myself and continued. And when I finished Rachel just sat there in stunned silence.

The first words out of her mouth were, "I knew you were too good to be true." She continued by apologizing to me for placing me on a pedestal, for "worshiping" me. She was so proud to be my wife and she had felt so secure and loved in our relationship. She was devastated but she reminded me she had promised to love me and to be with me until death. She said she was going to stand with me and, together, we would continue to fight this battle, turning to God more fervently as a couple.

She wanted to know if anybody else knew about this. I told her I had never shared it with anyone. She wondered if my parents had ever suspected anything, so I told her about some of my experiences, and also about the time my sister had found the bra; but no one, I assured her, really knew the depth of my problem. I had kept it to myself, fearing rejection, ridicule and that my life would be over if anyone ever found out.

But there was a fallout from the atomic bomb I dropped on Rachel that night; it was predictable. What other secrets had I kept from her? Could she trust me with our boys? Could she trust me, period? What was this going to mean and how was our life going to be impacted? What did I really want out of all this?

The answer was I didn't know. I didn't have answers to many of these questions, but I did know the answer to the one about whether she could trust me with the boys. It was an emphatic *Yes!* She could trust me, because I could never do anything to harm them. I loved them more than I loved my life.

More than these pressing questions, Rachel wondered if what we had was all a lie and a sham. Did all those wonderful memories of our first years together, the birth of our sons, their birthday parties, were all these just an act on my part? These suspicions tore me up, because I knew my answers would be met with skepticism and would not be believed. The absolute truth is that I cherish all these wonderful moments to this day. Though at the time I was going through hell on the inside, I was given the ability to be there *genuinely* for them.

Not long ago I was looking at our family photo albums and remembered this little thought that always ran through my head whenever I was aware my picture was about to be taken. I would say to myself, "It's okay, don't worry—the camera can't see the real you."

I was convinced that Rachel's lack of knowledge of my gender issues had been the missing piece of the puzzle. It made sense to me that God would now listen to my prayers, snap His fingers, and *voila!* I would be healed. That was my wishful thinking.

Soon after this crushing disclosure, Rachel learned one of her sisters in Texas had been diagnosed with breast cancer and was to undergo surgery soon. Rachel wanted to be there for her so she could help take care of the two young daughters. We planned for Rachel to go to Texas for up to one month.

There was more bad news that year: my brother Enrique was diagnosed with an inoperable brain tumor. He had been grocery shopping and was one block away from home when he passed out at the wheel of his VW van and crashed into a parked car. Fortunately, he was not traveling very fast and was not injured—just a little banged up. He was taken to the hospital by ambulance and discharged after the doctors concluded that he had not been eating well, and his blood sugar was low. A few months later he began to have seizures, and it was at this time he underwent further testing.

They performed a CAT scan and that's when the tumor was discovered. He was banned from driving until he was stabilized with anti-seizure medication.

It was during this time that I began to wonder if one option might not be for me to accommodate my "needs" somehow; to cross-dress from time to time as a relief valve. But I feared I was walking in a minefield by even contemplating such an idea. I had read an article in a magazine about a man who had been caught wearing his wife's clothes and she had decided to use this to her advantage. She blackmailed the husband to get her way in the marriage and basically reduced him to a slave. For example, the husband was expected to clean the house wearing dresses and aprons and was generally demeaned. The story pointed out the husband feigned protest but didn't really resist the treatment.

It was an appalling story that went against everything I believed constituted a healthy marriage. However, I gleaned a couple of things from this true story. One was I was not alone—there were other men with a similar "secret." (The article did not go into the man's history and he may not have been transgender; he could have been only a cross-dresser or a fetishist.) The other thing I learned was not all wives and significant others were turned off by this behavior.

Enrique had by now come into his faith with conviction, and had joined a church that had a ministry to the gay community. More correctly stated, it had a ministry to help individuals who wanted to leave the gay lifestyle. One of the lay ministers who helped in this particular work of the church operated a janitorial company, and my brother contracted them to do the cleaning at the restaurant. When I found out about the man's involvement in that ministry I decided to approach him one day and ask him if I could speak to him privately about something. I felt relatively safe doing so.

We made an appointment a few days later, and I confessed everything to him. He was unfazed by my admission and suggested that, if Rachel was agreeable, she might allow me to have some items to wear in the privacy of the bedroom in much the same way some couples incorporate sex toys into their love life. He opined these kinds of aids were morally neutral within the confines of a marriage relationship as long as they were mutually accepted and agreed upon. This was new information for me. I wondered about the wisdom of it, since I had spiritualized all facets of this and labeled them sinful. Did other "Christian" couples really do stuff like that?

Would our marriage survive if it were possible for me to accommodate my needs? If so, what were my needs? Again, the questions of who I was, and what I was, needed to be answered—but I was afraid to ask the question. More importantly, I feared the answer.

There was not much joy the day I drove Rachel and the boys down to Seattle for the flight to Dallas. (It was cheaper than flying from Vancouver and it would be a direct flight). Once we'd said our farewells at the airport Rachel broke my heart with her question. With a pained look on her face she looked into my eyes and asked if this was goodbye. I looked at her and answered, "I don't know."

I drove back to Vancouver broken, defeated and unsure of whether I could hang in there. I loved my wife and our sons beyond measure, but I just had no hope left in me. Why was I like this? Why couldn't I be normal? Was my faith not strong enough? What more could I do? A secret of any kind is, like cancer, a slow killer.

Chapter 21: Hitting Rock Bottom

I was haunted by Rachel's question, "Is this goodbye?" I didn't have an answer, because of all the doubt I had in my mind about my ability to keep it together. Was I being selfish by expecting her to love me unconditionally even though I might be imploding? What future did she have with me, and how were the boys going to be impacted? I had so many questions and so few answers.

Her time in Texas with the boys was to be our trial separation. I had to figure out if I was going to be able to uphold my end of the deal and stand by my promises to love and to cherish and to have no other besides her. We had always added to the end of our conversations about these kind of concerns, "...and divorce is not an option."

I debated whether it was unrealistic to accommodate my needs as had been suggested. Would it be opening up a Pandora's box to do this? I was sure about one thing: my problem wasn't going away; not even disclosing to Rachel had made any difference. I was so convinced that disclosing to her was the missing piece to the puzzle as to why my prayers for *healing* had not been answered. I just didn't get it, and felt hopeless.

I had never set out to get drunk for the sake of getting drunk enough to pass out. On the first week I spent alone in our empty little house I sat down with a bottle of rum and downed two large glasses full of the stuff, one after the other—about half the bottle. I refilled the glass and placed it on the side table. Then I leaned back on the couch, closed my eyes, and waited for the alcohol to do its magic.

My tolerance for alcohol was not very high, so it didn't take long but I didn't find out until I stood up to use the washroom and, oh boy, I was wobbly. I came back and downed the third glass. Then I lay down on the couch and cried myself to sleep—or until I passed out. Probably the latter.

I must've been out for about twelve hours, and when I awoke I was sick as a dog. I had alcohol poisoning. I felt as if a truck had rolled over me; this was no regular hangover. Although I had been able to turn off my brain for a few hours I recognized the futility of taking this direction. No amount of drinking or self-medicating was ever going to make *this* go away.

More devastating than this realization was the prospect of losing my wife and sons. I couldn't bear to look inside the tiny bedroom with the bunk beds. Sleeping in an empty bed myself was equally difficult, so I slept on the living room couch. I avoided coming home for as long as I could, as it was horrible to return to an empty house.

Of course, no one in my family was the wiser and had no idea of what Rachel and I were going through. As far as they were concerned, Rachel had gone to help her sister and that is all they ever asked about, "How is her sister? How are the boys doing and, "Is Rachel okay?" After a lifetime of learning how to act, how to pretend and always put the best face forward, I had no problem maintaining the expected "stable, caring and mature Jim" façade.

What a hypocrite I was. If I really allowed myself to fantasize, I pictured myself living as a woman and not giving a rat's ass about what anyone thought. But that wasn't me. I could never contemplate doing anything that would jeopardize my utter and complete dependence on being surrounded by those I love. But even more importantly than that, I didn't want to hurt anyone. Rachel had been gone over two weeks, yet it seemed like an eternity. I could not imagine life without her and our sons. I had hit rock bottom, and I knew in my heart what I had to do.

I had a couple of weeks vacation coming and Rachel and I had discussed the possibility of me driving down to Texas and bringing them home. This, of course, was based upon whether or not we were going to stay apart. I decided to surprise her and drove down in a couple of days. The drive itself was very therapeutic and gave me a lot of time to think things over, pleading with God for help. I don't know if I am the only one for whom this is true, but it is on long drives like this when I have negotiated with God and made promises in exchange for His favors. I know it sounds silly to put it that way but that's, in fact, what it is—a time to negotiate a new arrangement with God.

My father-in-law lived in a corner house with a gravel driveway that formed an "L" around the house. I entered the driveway from the side street and as I drove up I spotted our two sons playing in the backyard, which had a low chain-link fence around it. Our eyes met at the same time and they shouted, "Dad is here!" and ran to the gate. Seconds later, Rachel rushed out the back door. She had seen me drive up through the kitchen window. I jumped out of the car picked up my sons in both arms and hugged and kissed them. Then I got to embrace and hold Rachel once again. I had called her a few hours earlier so she knew about me coming, but it was a surprise to the boys. She had not told the boys I would be joining them at some point in case I didn't.

Rachel's sister was recovering well and it was time to get back to the business of living for us all. We visited with Rachel's grandparents, who lived just south of the Red River in a small farming community in east Texas. Then it was time to head home to try to put our lives back together again with a new determination to make things work. How this was going to look—or work—I had no idea.

Rachel also had a lot of time to think during our time apart. This was a private matter for her and she did not discuss any of this with anyone. In some ways I wish she had done so instead of keeping it all to herself. But this was Rachel, if before she'd harbored any doubts, those doubts were now banished in her resolve to make it work. She was prepared to make sacrifices and to do whatever it would take to stand by me and support me in my brokenness. Our coming together in Texas seemed to mark a new beginning for us. Maybe we had more realistic, readjusted expectations—yet I could not help but think that she was forcing herself to settle for second best.

I, on the other hand, was grateful for a second chance. Yet I couldn't help but feel as if I was on probation. My focus at home was to do everything I could to ensure our sons would have a normal and happy childhood. It would be untrue to say I did not intentionally use them as my distraction, since that is what they became. I was motivated by them to be the best dad I could be, even if I could not claim to be the best husband.

Our third son was born in May of 1983, nine months to the day of my surprise arrival in Texas. He is the legacy of our coming together once again.

Our eight hundred square foot house in Vancouver was feeling smaller and smaller every day. We had finished the basement, put in a playroom and added a second bathroom, but we knew the day was coming when we would have to find a house with more bedrooms.

By now our oldest son was in second grade and our middle son in playschool. Rachel was one of the few stay-at-home moms in our neighborhood, and was totally invested in our sons' lives. We had enrolled our oldest son in a bilingual French school which, unfortunately, was not in our immediate catchment area, so Rachel became the taxi service for him and some of his friends whose mothers worked.

Our involvement at church was becoming more and more sporadic. Not because of "my issue" but because it was too exhausting for us. Every Sunday we had to pack so much stuff, diapers, bottles, toys, etc. Then one of us would always have to help watch the children in the back room during the service. We were not enjoying the experience. It was easier to just stay home on Sundays.

The family's restaurant had been expanded and I had essentially trained myself out of a job. I had assumed kitchen responsibilities, which could be transferred to others for less pay than I would require. It made more sense for me to return to graphic design, and I was able to resume working for some of our previous clients. Enrique was more interested in helping to run the restaurant.

On top of all this activity, Enrique and I were approached by Capilano College to see if one of us would like to teach a course in the graphic design and illustration program. We were both so busy we asked if we could team-teach the course and proposed how the curriculum would work. Each week would be a different block and we would alternate every other week. The college accepted the proposal, and we became the tag team who taught "Studio Production."

Enrique had fallen in love with a Canadian woman he met while on vacation in Mexico soon after his diagnosis. They were engaged about the same time the doctors decided to operate on the tumor. Enrique's tumor was an *astrocytoma*—shaped like a star with a small nucleus and radiating tentacles. It is a difficult type of tumor to remove completely, since the core is relatively small and removing the tentacles can damage surrounding healthy brain tissue. Consequently, the surgeons just did a "sub-total" removal of his tumor.

With any brain surgery there is always the risk of physical or mental impairment. Fortunately Enrique was not affected physically; the only thing that changed was almost imperceptible: he became a little passive and was not as gung-ho about things as he had always been. Unless you knew him really well before the surgery, you would not have really noticed this mild change in his personality. He married his fiancée about six months after the surgery and the ensuing radiation treatments. Doctors were confident he would enjoy many more years of life.

The success of the Mexican restaurant was of interest to the Keg restaurants, which had been one of our original graphic design clients. I was doing a lot of design work for their vice-president, who oversaw the Washington State region, and we started talking one day about whether or not we were considering expansion of our restaurant. The Keg was prepared to finance a joint venture with our family, and, after much discussion, we decided to open a second location in downtown Vancouver. I was to be the general manager and president of the new joint venture company.

The new restaurant opened in September of 1984 and once again I stopped doing graphic design. I was also going to be so busy with the restaurant that I would not be able to team-teach in the fall semester, or possibly ever again. Enrique was willing to teach on his own, so that is what we did—I managed the second restaurant and he taught at the college and did office work with Dad at the first restaurant.

What can I tell you about how I was doing that won't bore you to death? Well, I'll tell you an anecdotal story that will give you a good idea. About ten years after this all took place, Rachel and I were looking at family pictures of the boys playing tee-ball, then Little League, and then at birthday parties. I remarked that I didn't remember some of those events. Rachel pointed out I didn't remember because I wasn't there—I was busy managing the restaurant downtown. It was true, I would come home after midnight and wake up after the boys had been taken to school. I hardly ever saw them. I tried to be at home as much as possible, but I realized Rachel was right—even though I thought I was doing a good job as a dad, I missed out on a lot.

You shouldn't be surprised I was not doing well privately. My busy schedule had subconsciously become my opiate. I was coping by allowing myself to possess some articles of clothing I could wear under my male clothing without detection. Rachel did not support or condone this but she reluctantly accepted it as the price to pay for being married to me. My hope for being free of the "bondage" had become non-existent by this time.

The year ended on a very bad note. On the Friday before Christmas, the last day of class at the college, Enrique did not show up for class. The department dean called me about 2:00 P.M. to ask if Enrique was alright because he had not come to class and he had failed to turn in the last grades to the office. She explained the college had been calling his house all day but there was no answer. She was very worried because of his condition.

I thanked her for calling and then called my parents to tell them I was rushing to Enrique's house. On the way, I feared he had taken his life because his marriage had not succeeded and I figured he might be depressed, given the time of the year. After knocking on his doors and windows and not getting a response, I decided to break in through a window when he suddenly appeared. He had come to see what all the noise was; he had been sleeping and looked awful.

I asked him if he was okay and he said he had been having insomnia for almost a week. He and I wondered if he could be needing his medications adjusted. When I explained he had missed class and the dean had called me he was really upset with himself. We called the college to report to the dean and she was most understanding. I then called Mom and Dad to tell them he was okay and they called his doctor immediately. He was given an appointment for first thing Monday morning. The doctor instructed them not to leave him unattended and not to let him drive. Mom and Dad came by and took him to their home for the weekend.

The news on Monday was not good. His tumor had grown and it had now worked its tentacles deeper into the brain. His doctor gave him six months and explained what we could expect. Because of where the tumor was located, Enrique would become more and more passive, would want to sleep more often and for longer periods, and would eventually slip into a coma.

Enrique died six months later, in June, 1985, at my parents' home, where he was cared for during the entire time. My mom would not contemplate the idea of his being alone in a hospital. She took care of him with the help of health care nurses. All of us visited and spent time with him as much as we could, given our crazy schedules.

The restaurant business was all-consuming, and I felt guilty for not being able to come by more often. On my way home in the early hours of the morning I would drive down the street, stop in front of my parents' house, look up to his bedroom window and say a prayer. I didn't want him to die.

It is very hard for me to admit this, but the truth is I envied him, and resented God for taking him instead of me. "Why not me, Lord? Take me and spare my brother." It seemed to me that would have been fairer.

Chapter 22: Fear of Falling

A parent's sorrow over the death of a child is immeasurable and unimaginable. I'll never forget the time my Dad drove Enrique to one of his appointments with the neurologist at the hospital. They were waiting in the reception area, when the receptionist came up to my dad and said the doctor could see him now. She had assumed, quite logically, that Dad was the patient, since he was the older of the two. Dad explained the appointment was for his son—and then he broke down. Dad felt the same way I did. It made more sense if it was he to be the one dying first.

Through it all, we were able to see a most beautiful side of our parents' love during those six months. They devoted themselves completely to Enrique and, by extension, to all of us. We, too, could expect them to be there for us in the same loving way.

A sudden death, I suspect, is much harder on loved ones—it comes as a shock. Enrique's prolonged death had given us a chance to process the loss gradually, and at the end we all wanted it to be over for him so that he would be freed from his failing body. My faith had been weak, but it was somehow strengthened by Enrique's faith. On one of my visits I asked him if he thought about death, and he answered, "I think about death all the time. But I am not afraid, I know where I am going, and I am looking forward to getting there." How our roles had reversed. He had looked to me for spiritual guidance, and now I was coming to him. I, too, thought about death all the time, and at times I thought it would solve so many of my problems.

We all mourned differently. My mother had the most visible sorrow, followed by my dad. They now had lost one son and, as I watched them, I wondered how they would be affected if anything happened to me.

Since I was the executor of my brother's estate it fell upon me to contact his ex-wife when I received the checks for the life insurance. That was all she was entitled to, based on the separation and divorce agreement. She arrived at my office with a new boyfriend. I thought that was so incredibly tactless. She was giddy—as if she had won the lottery. Had this been her motive for marrying my brother? Was she just a gold digger? I was so disgusted.

There have been many times when I have had to do things beyond my capabilities. Being Enrique's executor was one of them. Jesus' words have been true—His grace has been sufficient during challenging times. For me, there is no other explanation that makes sense to me. Had I done this on my own strength I would have wilted and shriveled up.

The year 1985 was difficult for all of us, and it was made the sadder for Rachel. Her sister's cancer had spread. She passed away a few days before Christmas.

There were other stresses for us in our business. Our partners in the second restaurant were being forced to consolidate and restructure their company. They had overextended themselves and we were left holding the bag at a time when the new operation needed help the most. They sold us their share for $1. Carmen and her husband decided to take over the new restaurant and assume the liabilities; I returned to full-time graphics.

After Enrique's death, I returned to teach the college course by myself the following September. I taught for two more years, then resigned. I closed the office and sold off or gave away most of the furnishings. I purchased a Macintosh computer when Apple introduced the LaserWriter and Aldus introduced PageMaker, and worked out of the basement under my family's restaurant.

Back in 1976, I came into our office in Gastown one day, Enrique was standing proudly next to a computer terminal with a tiny green screen. The case had plywood sides, and the keyboard was in a clunky extruded aluminum enclosure. Next to it was a rubber coupling device, where the telephone receiver was placed as soon as you heard a high pitched squeal. An enterprising high school teacher had developed a very basic accounting program with General Ledger and Accounts Receivable and Payable modules. The scheme was the teacher rented computer time from the mainframe at the University of Alberta, and then rented out terminals to small businesses so they could computerize their accounting.

When we got this machine Enrique was thrilled. He logged in once a week for half an hour (the allotted time for us), and two days later we would get a stack of large computer paper about four inches thick, bound in pale blue card stock covers held together with plastic spindles. According to Enrique, everything we ever wanted to know about our company was right there at our fingertips. The only problem was leafing through that stack of pages to find the information we were looking for!

My eyes glazed over when I saw that thing. Fortunately, it was he who did the accounting and administration, while I was the purist, the artist. Fast forward a few years, and Enrique was visualizing and predicting the day when we would no longer have drafting tables but, instead, would sit in front of a computer screen to do our work. Clearly, by 1985, that day had come. Enrique's prediction about the computer as a graphic design tool was starting to come true.

For the next two years I think I was in denial: I felt unhinged and very vulnerable after Enrique's death. The responsibilities of being a husband, father, and sole breadwinner were taking their toll. As I approached my fortieth birthday in 1990, I knew I needed professional help. I tried to survive the best way I could, privately and secretly, and feared a breakdown. I feared that suddenly my thoughts would no longer be private, and my secret would all be made public. I agonized about the impact this would have on my sons, and, most of all, on Rachel. The years since I disclosed to her had also taken an incredible toll on her. She was always loving and supportive, but I knew she lived with disappointment and resignation. How I wished I could have spared her so much pain.

Many years earlier, when our oldest son started playing T-ball, we got to meet some of the other parents. There was a couple who alternated coming to the games—they were divorced. The reason for the breakup of their marriage was the father, a medical doctor, had "come out" as gay. To see a psychiatrist I needed a referral, and, since I was too embarrassed to go to our own family doctor, I decided a gay doctor would be more understanding. I called his office and made an appointment to see if he would be willing to make the referral. Gratefully he did, but even so, it was hard to admit to him the reason why I felt I needed professional help. He understood completely.

I had three sessions with the psychiatrist, during which he skillfully helped me to verbalize my conflicting thoughts. Being able to finally spew out the stuff after all these years was a good thing to do. These sessions also helped me explain things to Rachel. After each session she would ask how it had gone, and what we had talked about. I was able to report things objectively and openly. In our final session the doctor offered to refer me to the Gender clinic at Vancouver General Hospital, but I refused his offer. I thanked him for helping me understand things. For now, he had diffused the time bomb.

Armed with this new information I felt I knew how to be more effective in my prayer life. I was going to fight the battle harder than I ever had before! I could not even begin to contemplate what the psychiatrist had proposed and, with Rachel's help, was more determined to stay the course. I still felt this was a spiritual battle, and knowing Satan's tactics was going to make the difference in the fight.

Chapter 23: Cocoon Time

In 1991 I accepted an invitation to be the in-house designer for a group of my client's restaurants that had merged. The principals, as well as many of the people in management, had worked for the Keg 'n' Cleaver restaurants in the seventies when Enrique and I were working on that account. To avoid a conflict of interest, I had to curtail my freelance activities with respect to other restaurants, but was allowed to keep my other clients, which was a small part of my business.

This arrangement was mutually beneficial for both parties. The new restaurant group would enjoy the benefit of having their designer within reach and available to them at all times. The biggest benefit to me was that I had a consistent, guaranteed income with benefits, something I had not enjoyed since I stopped working at our family's restaurant.

This arrangement simplified my life considerably, since I would not have to be generating so many invoices and managing the accounts receivable, something I had always found stressful. Enrique had always done the accounting and the few years during the few years we worked together, I missed him terribly. In California, I was his little brother, a clingy pest. In Canada, though, we got to know each other as adults, and got along really well, especially after he embraced his faith and we had that in common—a true brotherly, earthly and spiritual bond.

I don't know how my brother would have received the news that I was transgender. He never knew anything about my struggles, because that's how I wanted it to be. I hid it from him and everyone else, and no one ever suspected anything. Not family; not friends; not clients. Nobody.

The new restaurant company went public soon after I joined, and this allowed it to expand very rapidly. What started out as a group of three restaurant concepts with a total of seven restaurant locations soon became seven concepts with over thirty locations. I was part of the marketing team, which was made up entirely of attractive women. Though I immersed myself in the work and loved what I did for a living, the close proximity to these women was absolute torture. I was not attracted to them, nor "lusted" for them, but because I had to work with them every day, they were a constant reminder of what I physically was not.

This new job coincided with our moving to a new church that had a larger youth contingent of similar ages to our two youngest sons. The church we had been going to had lots of young families with very young children, and older, mostly retired, couples. However, couples our age seemed to be missing, due to their exodus from Vancouver-proper to the suburbs, where family housing was more affordable. Our oldest son was no longer interested in coming to church with us, but the two younger ones still took part. We were concerned they were often the only ones their age in Sunday school or at church events.

I had become involved in worship, and really appreciated the many new contemporary worship songs coming from such groups as the *Vineyard Fellowship* churches. I was finding strength and encouragement in many of these new lyrics, which resonated within my heart and expressed my yearnings and my love for God in a new, fresh, and powerful way. These songs allowed me to focus on God with an intimacy I had never experienced before. The best way to describe my prayer life before is that I *had* no prayer life, I could never really "stay on the line" long enough to have a meaningful conversation with God.

In the comic strip *Family Circus* there was a recurring story-line which showed the backyard or the inside of the house with a dotted line that went all over the place. I remember one in particular;

the mom asks the little boy to go tell Daddy that dinner is ready. So he starts in the kitchen, goes out the back door, swings on the tire hanging from the tree, runs around the tree, gets on his bike rides it a short distance, hops off and picks up a ball, bounces it for a bit and, after several of these detours, enters a garage to give his father the message. That's what it seemed like when I prayed.

I'd start out focused on one topic, but before I knew it I'd be thinking about something I saw in the news, or some job I was working on, and then something else—and before long I was not praying anymore. I would return in my mind to prayer, and apologize to God for being so rude, only to find myself repeating this pattern. It doesn't matter if I'm in a darkened room, or in a very special place set aside for prayer, I've just never been able to pray fervently the way some people claim they can. Worship music, on the other hand, allows me to focus on God, to express my love, my pain and my gratitude, without losing my train of thought.

This was another reason why we felt at home in the new church; they, too, had a focus on this type of worship. We were introduced to this church by our friends George and Ann, a couple we met at Dayspring Fellowship in the late seventies. They had four girls, three of whom were similar in age to our three boys.

When the children were little, Rachel would get together with Ann; their kids and ours grew up almost as brothers and sisters. Their whole family was very musical, and both parents were part of the worship team. Since we had that in common it was natural for me to join the worship team with them. And, as we were new at church, they suggested we should attend their Bible study group, which met every other week at a couple's house. The group consisted of about a dozen people, some single, mostly married, of all ages.

Coincidently, one of the couples was the retired pastor and his wife from First Baptist Church, whom we had met when we first got married and who were still somewhat involved at the Hobbit House.

Their son was the pastor of this new church. Small world!

For the next few years, this was our life. I had a full-time job I loved that kept me busy, Rachel had a part-time job working for the Vancouver School Board, and we were both trying to create healthy memories with our boys.

By this time my battle with the enemy was at a stalemate. I had dug trenches, but there were no victories—just the resignation that my issue was here to stay. As a result of my sessions with the psychiatrist, I entertained the thought I might be transgender, but I still could not allow myself to make the claim; it would have been admitting defeat. But as time passed, this seemed to be the only explanation that made sense. It scared me.

Five years after I joined the restaurant company there had been a large influx of new people in management, and all the loyalties I had enjoyed with the original operators were disappearing one by one. I got to see firsthand how the changing of the guard can influence corporate culture, and it became harder to see a long-term future for me there.

I was able to leave on good terms, and retained much of the work I was doing for the company anyway. I now worked from home full-time and not dealing with people face-to-face every day. This was both good and bad. The good included the benefits of the short commute from the bedroom to the office down the hall, but I missed the positive reinforcement I enjoyed while I was working in-house. People appreciated my work and my contribution, and I got a lot of satisfaction from this. (Rachel might add my sitting at home alone for hours on end also left me vulnerable to my own thoughts and needs.)

A few years earlier the family sold the restaurant company so Dad and Mom could retire. They offered any of us the option to pay for the business over time since none of us had the means to buy them out. They needed and wanted to retire, however, so we insisted it would be best if we found an outside buyer, so they could get their money out once and for all. The restaurant had been good to us, and its success made us proud of what we had accomplished as a family.

Life continued to unfold, but by 1998 I had reached another low and, once again, feared a breakdown. Thanks to the Internet, I was able to carry out private research and, in doing so, became more and more convinced I might be transgender. I needed to know for sure, so I contacted the Gender clinic at Vancouver General Hospital to find out what I had to do to make an appointment. I was told I needed to be referred by my doctor; that was the only way they could see me.

I didn't think it would be possible for me to do this with our family doctor. He had delivered all three of our sons, and I was just too embarrassed to approach him with a request for the referral. I decided to call the clinic one more time and ask them if they could give me the name of a doctor who was sympathetic to transgender people, someone who had referred other patients in the past. The receptionist gave me the name and phone number of a physician.

I called the doctor's office immediately to make an appointment; fortunately, he was accepting new patients. It was time for me to have a physical anyway, and this gave me a good excuse to make the appointment. I was totally candid with him when we met, and explained to him how I had gotten his name. He agreed to write the referral letter, and promised to call me as soon as there was an open date for me at the clinic.

Chapter 24: Gender Clinic

All my adult life, from the time I was twenty years old, I had viewed my issue as being a spiritual one. My reason for becoming a Christian was not without a large measure of hope that God was going to make me normal. The insidious persistence of my negative self "male" image often made me question my faith. My linear, legalistic and fundamentalist approach served more to make me feel defeated than liberated. Nothing had worked, and nothing made sense.

On the other hand, my faith had infused my life with blessings. Top among them was meeting my wife. My faith also helped set me on a journey alongside people with whom I enjoyed an incredible sense of intimacy and kinship, which was peculiar. What I mean by that is that *fellowship* happened with a most eclectic and disparate collection of persons who, without their faith bond, would never have found themselves becoming friends with each other. At times I have experienced a level of genuine love and care from "total strangers" that has felt as strong as the love I have for my family.

More than all of these things, my faith has allowed me to experience intimacy with God, and that intimacy has given me the confidence to approach Him without fear.

The words of Jesus that resonated with me as a child and teenager when I heard them read in Mass were seminal in my hope to be fixed. (Coincidentally, the first time I read *The Sermon on the Mount* after my "conversion" experience, I discovered most of those gems came from these sayings.) His warnings and exhortations—to not judge lest you be judged; where your treasure is, there will your heart be also; if any one asks you to go one mile, go with him two—influenced my values and my view on life.

The Beatitudes moved me to tears, because they were central to my hope for His miracle. "Blessed are the poor in spirit, for theirs is the kingdom of heaven. Blessed are those who mourn, for they shall be comforted ..." These became central to my view on life and produced a hunger that was only satisfied by placing myself at His mercy. My faith had also protected me; it kept me sober, kept me from inflicting myself with self-destructive behaviors, addictions, suicide.

Contradictory as it may seem, though I failed to be fixed, I grew closer to God. And now I found myself at a crossroad. What now?

I approached my first appointment at the gender clinic with a mixture of skepticism and suspicion. This was a "secular" institution, and in that sense I felt as if I was stepping out of the "spiritual" camp to seek help for something I still viewed as a spiritual problem. But part of me was being more pragmatic. Wasn't medicine a "gift" from God? Couldn't one see the advancement of knowledge in all areas of the human condition as a gift to be received with gratitude?

In one of the sessions at the clinic I had made the comment that at times I thought it would be better for all if I just ended it. The counselor stopped me and said, "I don't know your family and I don't know any of your friends. But if it were possible for me to survey every single one of your family members and every one of your friends and asked them, 'Would you rather Jim live the rest of his life as a woman or for him to not be here at all?' I guarantee you one hundred percent of the responses would be they would rather have you live as a woman. So don't go there. You don't strike me as the kind of person who would want to inflict untold pain on your loved ones, and that is what you would be doing if you chose to end it all." He was right. I am forever grateful for that bit of wisdom.

The assessment at the clinic lasted about six months. At the end the psychiatrist gave me his and the team's conclusion: I had a condition known as gender dysphoria. Dysphoria is the polar opposite to euphoria, which is extreme ecstasy. This explanation resonated with me—I had extreme sadness about my gender. The doctor went on to explain how the Gender clinic could help me make the necessary changes in my life to transform and live successfully as a woman. Whatever assistance I was to receive would follow the Harry Benjamin Standards of Practice for the treatment of transsexuals. This protocol would help insure my transition would be carefully monitored and supervised. The choice was left to me to decide whether or not I was ready, and willing, to begin down this path.

This diagnosis was both a blessing and a curse: a blessing because at last I knew what I was; it offered an explanation for all the confusion I had lived with all my life. But it was a curse, too, as it was a life sentence, and the options open to me were impossible for me to consider.

I could not begin to entertain what transitioning would do to my marriage and family. I was so fearful of rejection and ridicule— and of being different! I had lived with this kind of fear all my life, but now I was even more frightened. I wondered what would happen when I told my clients. Would they stop using me as their designer? What would my friends think and do? How was my church going to respond? Would I be ostracized, or would I be embraced?

I left my last appointment mostly disappointed. I had hoped the doctors would be able to suggest a therapy or medication that would alleviate my burden, yet I knew it was pointless to think so. There was no magic bullet.

Rachel attended one of the sessions with me. It was difficult for her to accept what she was hearing, and what I was reporting to her every time I came home after one of my sessions. She often repeated that the clinic simply had a cookie-cutter approach, and that I didn't have to accept everything they said as the truth. She pleaded with me to simply keep trusting in God, that with her help, love, and support, we would get through this, and all would be okay. She added I could dress as I wanted in the privacy of our bedroom, that she understood

I had this need, but to never wear anything in front of the boys.

My fear of rejection and scorn from my church was not altogether unfounded. Do you remember the couple that invited us to join the church, the one with the four daughters? At one of the home group Bible studies we attended while I was being assessed, Ann shared a prayer request with the group. She explained her older brother had started to live as a woman and 'he-she' was being selfish and self-centered, jeopardizing his marriage and the welfare of his children, and how upset she was with him for doing this.

I don't know what went through Rachel's mind, but the group's reaction troubled me. With the exception of the retired pastor's wife, everyone thought how horrible it was, tisked and shook their heads in disapproval. The retired pastor's wife was the only one who made a comment that was compassionate. She said quietly to herself, "Oh, the poor guy. I wonder what his life has been like?" I was disappointed that more people had not responded in like manner.

The group's reaction did not bode well for me. I could expect them to react the same way if I ever came out. Therefore, I would never come out. That was the only safe conclusion.

As we were grabbing our coats and getting ready to leave the Bible study, Ann turned to me and with a tongue-in-cheek tone asked me, "You don't have any transgender people in your family, do you?" Ha-ha, how funny, I thought. If she only knew.

At the gender clinic, I had been given a handout that listed several support groups catering to transgender individuals and their significant others. Rachel had no desire for any of this, and I was reluctant to go public anywhere for fear of the cat being let out of the bag. What if I was recognized?

One of the groups was described as a social group for crossdressers and transgender individuals. They met once a month and one was free to attend, presenting as either male or female, but most people attended in their "chosen" gender. The group was not intended for transsexuals or individuals who were "living full-time."

When I called the phone number listed, I got a recording. After all, this was an all-volunteer organization. It asked for a name and phone number and a brief message explaining what was wanted or needed, and the call would be returned within twenty-four hours. I hung up the phone because I didn't want them calling and having one of my sons answer the phone. After doing some thinking, I called again, and this time left my information, requesting that I only be called between certain hours to ensure I would be the only one home.

When the person called back, I asked a lot of questions about the group, and was told the process for joining it. Because they wanted to maintain a high level of confidentiality, all people who attended had to first be screened in an interview. The group also wanted to ensure the individuals who came were not just looking for sexual contacts and services.

It felt very clandestine when I met for lunch with the person who was in charge of membership. He was thirty-one years old, and quite open about his lifestyle and involvement in this group. He often went out in public as a woman, but was still in the closet with respect to his family and friends. This was his secret life. Here I was face-to-face with someone who was a bona fide cross-dresser/transgender individual. He gave me an application to fill out, and told me to mail it in and I would know in short order if I had been accepted. I never did send in the application. I was just too afraid to go public, even with these individuals who had as much to lose as I did if there was ever a breach of confidence.

Ann's brother, who was living as a woman and went by the name Monica, eventually separated from his wife and began a life on her own. These friends became a test tube for me. I watched and listened, paying close attention anytime he-she was mentioned in conversation. I finally got to meet her brother-sister at the wedding of one of their daughters. He presented as male for that occasion and everyone addressed him by his male name. He looked somewhat androgynous but not over-the-top. I noted tolerance rather than acceptance of this individual. He was there with his ex-wife, but there was a distance between them.

Then, as each of their daughters got married a few years apart, I got to see a gradual transformation of this person. I also witnessed how the family treated her, and heard what they said about her, which was usually not very complimentary. At one of the weddings the joke among the younger people was to "Find Aunt Monica," a clear take off on "Find Waldo." I found the joke to be insensitive and cruel. I feared this is what I could expect for myself if I ever came out. Would I be willing to pay that kind of price?

"Never!" I would say to myself.

Chapter 25: A Disaster and a Wedding

Sometime in June of 2006, as all the details were coming together for our oldest son's wedding in September, I received an email from our middle son that suddenly threatened to derail the occasion. He was very angry with me, accused me of being a hypocrite, and questioned what kind of a Christian I was. He went on to say he had learned some very disturbing things about me, and as a result was breaking off contact. He didn't want me to call or email him.

I knew immediately that he must have seen some of the web pages I had bookmarked in my computer that dealt with transsexualism and transgender issues. His reaction devastated me, and I wondered how his demand for breaking off all contact was going to impact his brother's wedding, since he was going to be the Master of Ceremonies. We had a family crisis on our hands.

When Rachel arrived home from work, I showed her the email, and she was very upset with me for being so careless. Though I had tried calling him several times that day and got no answer, she called him using her cell phone and he answered. Rachel insisted on seeing him right away and left as soon as she hung up the phone.

She was gone for a good three hours during which I just felt sick to my stomach. I am not surprised he might have seen some images he found disturbing. Some of the forums I had visited had links to all kinds of pornographically explicit photos of "she-males," men who have feminized their bodies but have retained the male working parts.

The fact is, when doing a search on the Internet using the keywords "transgender" or "transsexual," the majority of the links are, unfortunately, pornographic in nature. I would sometimes bookmark a page planning to come back later to read it more carefully. As I was waiting for Rachel to come home I examined some of these book-marked pages and I could see why he had found them disturbing. Rachel was right, I should have been more careful.

Now the damage was done. I played out all kinds of possible scenarios in my head. Maybe it was good it happened, I thought to myself. Was it time to disclose my secret to my sons and my family? Is he going to boycott the wedding? Will he refuse to attend if I am there? If so, how is this going to be explained to the rest of the family—and what will the new in-laws think? How I wished at that moment I could have rolled back the clock so that I could have prevented this.

When Rachel got home, she did not want to go into details. What she told him was I had a coping issue, I was always under a lot of stress, I was a good man, and for him to think what a good Dad I had been to him. But she didn't explain anything to him about my having a medical condition, and what it meant. She told me he needed time to process things, and to wait for him to come to me. How I wished he would have done so and asked me for an explanation instead of jumping to the worst conclusions. It was horrible.

I saw my son for the first time since he cut me off on the night of the rehearsal. He was pleasant and polite, but he was not in a talkative mood with me. All I was able to say to him was we needed to talk and to please come to me when he was ready. I was so grateful for how he rose to the occasion on the wedding day. He was kind and loving, and I knew it was hard for him to put on a good face. But he did.

As I have already shared, the month of October is a busy month in our family with regard to special days. It's my mom's birthday, my parents' and our wedding anniversaries, and Canadian Thanksgiving. Our middle son boycotted all of those family events and, when others asked him if he was coming, he would fabricate some excuse. The same thing happened in November for my birthday, and at Christmas he arrived late for dinner and only stayed a short time. Obviously he was still processing and he was still upset. Everyone asked us if there was something wrong with him, if he was okay.

Were my worst fears being realized? Was this just a taste of things to come; were people going to judge and ostracize me the way my son had? Things didn't look good.

By this time I had come to accept my diagnosis. You've probably heard this story or a version of it:

A man falls overboard in the middle of the ocean and prays to God for a miracle. After a while, a fishing boat comes up to the man and the fishermen try to help him on board. But he refuses to be picked up by them, saying he is expecting a miracle from God. Next, a Coast Guard rescue boat comes to his aid but again refuses help because he is expecting a miracle. Finally, a helicopter arrives on the scene but he waves it away. A few hours later, exhausted by now, he drowns. When he gets to heaven he demands to speak to God about his untimely death. The man is ushered into God's presence and asks why God let him drown. God looks at the man and says, "What do you mean 'let you drown?' I sent you a fishing boat, the Coast Guard and a helicopter but you refused my help! That's why you drowned."

In some ways this little parable described me. It dawned on me one day that perhaps God was answering my prayer, but that I had been so focused on how I thought it was going to look I failed to see He was answering it in a completely different way than I had expected. The fact I lived at a time and in a place where my condition was understood—was that not an answer to prayer? There were now people who were trained and available to help me navigate these uncharted waters—was that not an answer to prayer? Would I be like the man in the story who failed to see how God had, in fact, made it possible for him to be rescued?

Now my biggest anxiety was how I was ever going to be able to pass as a female, given I now had a receding hairline and a beard that produced a five-o'clock shadow by 3:00 p.m. every day. Though I was an avid jogger and ran three times a week, I was still packing a fair amount of excess weight. How was I ever going to pull it off?

The other obstacle to overcome had nothing to do with my ability to pass in public. It had to do with how my parents would take the news. Dad was already close to ninety, and Mom a few years younger. Should I just hold off on everything and wait until both of them passed away? Rachel would often stress this as the reason for why I should put the idea of transitioning completely out of my mind.

After much introspection, I decided to begin doing things that would not draw a lot of attention to myself. I started by doing longer runs whenever I jogged, doing stomach crunches on a daily basis, and I started electrolysis to gradually reduce my beard. Within six months I had lost fifteen pounds and gone from a thirty-four to a thirty-one inch waist. By July of 2007, I had come down a total of 25 pounds and my waist was now under thirty inches. People were now noticing there was something different—especially my mother—who asked every time she saw me if I was okay. In her opinion, I was too skinny. None of my clothes fit any more, and I looked like I was wearing borrowed clothing. I had also endured close to one hundred and fifty hours of electrolysis—and to my disappointment, it looked like I still had as many more hours to go.

You might ask why I was doing this, especially after I tell you I had not yet contacted the Gender clinic to tell them I was ready to begin the prescribed process. The reason was I wanted to be ready. When I was diagnosed and the protocol explained to me, I was told I would have to start living as a woman immediately—even before starting hormone therapy. I remember telling the doctor there was no way I could do that. I said to him, "Look at me, I can't pass as a woman. I would be a joke! If I go out in public, I will be spotted in an instant." This was one of the deal breakers then. This time I wanted to have a better chance of pulling it off.

I called Vancouver General Hospital when I was unable to find the phone number for the gender clinic. That's when I learned the clinic had been closed, and there was now a new arrangement called the Trans-Health Program. Basically, the clinic had fallen victim to government budget cuts and it was a trimmed down version now.

I called the new office, and explained I had been a patient about eight years earlier, diagnosed as a transsexual, and though had not then proceeded with any changes, was ready to do so now. The receptionist entered my name into the computer, and informed me that my records had been archived since I had not been in contact with the clinic for more than three years. I was instructed to call the General Hospital's records office to request my records be released to the Clinic. This would take up to three months since it was not an emergency.

I was relieved in some ways about this delay. I was scared as hell, and had no idea what they were going to say to me this time around. I could not bring myself to tell Rachel I had contacted the clinic. She knew I was up to something, having lost all the weight and facial hair, but I think she thought I was simply doing this to help me cope better. I did not want to do things behind her back, but the fact was she didn't want to discuss anything having to do with my diagnosis. In this regard, communication was nonexistent.

Chapter 26: What Will People Think?

"What will people think?" I've discovered this question can never be adequately answered, ever.

I became very paranoid about being seen going in and out of the Clinic, the doctors' offices and medical labs I was now having to visit on a regular basis. Our church has many members who work in health sciences, and since I didn't know where any of them worked, I was always on the lookout as I entered and left the medical buildings.

I worried that if people found out about me, the discovery would embroil our church in controversy. I knew one individual who was very critical of anything that hinted at the acceptance of gays. One Sunday during a pastoral prayer there was a request on behalf of victims of violence due to their race, color, creed, gender or sexual orientation. That week he railed into the pastor, members of the deacons' board, and anyone who crossed his path. Since when did we start to look favorably on gays? My, oh my, was this individual incensed or what? I was one of the unlucky ones he dumped on. All I could think of at the time was, "Well, brother, you ain't heard nothing yet!"

A few years earlier, some members had left our church because the new assistant minister, who was female, presented too "butch," and they thought this was wrong. When they lost the vote at the confirmation meeting they protested with their feet. Granted, they were only two or three individuals, but they certainly did not like the fact so many stood up for this young woman and voted for her.

Aware of the potential damage that could result if my disclosure was not handled correctly, I decided it was time to step down from my involvement in the worship team. Towards the end of September, 2007, the worship leaders got together to discuss and plan the music for the Advent and Christmas seasons. The pastor chaired the meeting and, like all other meetings we'd ever had, this one was sprinkled with laughter and warm camaraderie. We all got along and worked together really well; no one had an ego—and I've seen some egos when it comes to worship leaders. So it took the pastor by surprise when I met with him a few weeks later to resign from all my responsibilities on the worship team.

We met one morning and over coffee I told him everything. I explained I was worried about being recognized entering or leaving a specialist's office by someone from church, about people jumping to conclusions without having all the facts. I did not want to cause a rift in the congregation; neither did I want to become the elephant in the room. Most of all, I did not want to become the poster child for transgender issues, or a cause célèbre. I reminded him of how some people had been upset during the hiring of the assistant minister, and opined my issue had a much larger potential for making things uncomfortable for him and the Deacons' Board.

Admittedly, this is what I said to him, but it wasn't easy for me to get the words out; my heart was in my throat, and I had to stop and compose myself throughout my disclosure. Have you ever been so nervous you can't stop talking? I think that was me that morning. I was absolutely terrified the pastor was going to judge me and exact his godly wrath on me.

He just sat there and listened to me, handing me extra napkins to wipe my eyes, and waited for me to finish. I'll never forget his first words, and the way he said them, full of compassion. He told me this was not a moral issue any more than being born with a physical disability or any other medical condition.

He thanked me for sharing with him and told me this did not disqualify me as a worship leader, adding it made me more qualified because of my integrity and honesty. Then he suspected, quite correctly, that I had been beating myself up all my life with scripture, and assured me he did not judge me. He was very concerned for Rachel and how this had affected her; he sympathized with her and what she must be going through.

When would I begin to make changes in my appearance, he wondered, and when was I planning to start presenting as female? I explained to him some of the changes that were already taking place. And, to the question of when I would start presenting as female, I told him he didn't have anything to worry about, it might not be for one or two years, or longer. I told them as long as my parents were alive I would most likely not take that step.

He then said something to me I will never forget: he promised me if I ever came to church as female he would stand with me and affirm me as a member of the congregation. As we were saying good-bye he asked me if I would like him to let the rest of the worship team know about my resignation or if I wanted to do that myself. He promised this information would be absolutely confidential between the two of us; he would not say anything to anyone about my reasons for stepping down. I was so grateful for his offer, I accepted—I could not see how I could possibly speak to all those people.

It must be said I was able, finally, to reconcile my faith to my condition, thanks to my pastor's first sermon as our new minister in which he set the tone for his style of teaching. He warned us then if we were looking for black and white dogmatic answers from him we were going to be disappointed. He explained, having been a diligent student of the Bible for close to twenty-five years, that he had come to the conclusion that no one had the right to pull out one or two verses of it to formulate a doctrine.

He told us we needed to approach the Bible with humility, recognizing the Bible itself is ambiguous, if not silent, on most aspects of the human condition. To compound the challenge, he asked how many times Jesus answered His questioners with ambiguity? How many times did He leave His listeners with more questions than they had before? Therefore, the pastor told us, we needed to be open to different points of view as we try to make sense of scripture and how it should be applied to life.

His sermon that day breathed life into my soul. I had always struggled with Jesus' comments recorded in chapter nineteen of the Gospel of Matthew. Jesus was having a discussion with His disciples about divorce and marriage and quoted the passage from chapter one of the book of Genesis that we often hear at weddings:

"Haven't you read," he replied, "that at the beginning the Creator 'made them male and female,' and said, 'For this reason a man will leave his father and mother and be united to his wife, and the two will become one flesh'? So they are no longer two, but one. Therefore what God has joined together, let man not separate."

The disciples were perplexed by his answer to the Pharisees, then he added this, which seemed out-of-the-blue:

"Not all men can accept this statement, but only those to whom it has been given. For there are eunuchs who were born that way from their mother's womb; and there are eunuchs who were made eunuchs by men; and there are also eunuchs who made themselves eunuchs for the sake of the kingdom of heaven. He who is able to accept this, let him accept it."

Now, tell me the last comment makes any sense to you if the discussion is about divorce and marriage. For years I used the first part of this passage, with its reference to Genesis, to beat myself up. I would often castigate myself with this rationale: "It says we are either male or female, there is no other option. Why do you allow yourself to go there in your thinking? Get it out of your mind, you are male! You have fathered three children, what more proof do you need?"

Then, gradually, after the pastor's sermon, I began to see something in Jesus' last statement I had never seen before. First, Jesus restated God created us male and female—but, He concedes, it doesn't always work out that way. Some are eunuchs because they are born that way.

In this one statement Jesus tells us it *isn't* all black and white. There are individuals who are *neither* male nor female; they are eunuchs, or inter-sexed, somewhere in between. We are, therefore, not to view gender and sex strictly as one or the other, but as a continuum with many aberrations and manifestations. Doing so only causes some to be marginalized ostracized, hated, and even persecuted.

Doctors and the parents of an intersex child have a difficult time deciding how to best raise that child. They will often make a decision one way or another, to raise a girl or a boy. The deciding factor might simply be a cultural preference, or what the parents feel they want in terms of gender. Unfortunately, studies show in fifty percent of the cases, as that child gets older and becomes more sexually self aware, the sex chosen for the child is at odds with the child's gender identity. If this is the case for a person born with "ambiguous" genitalia—that their gender identity is not directly related to their biological sexual characteristics—then who has the right to draw any lines of delineation as to which gender and sex pairings are correct?

This thought or understanding didn't come to me all at once; it was as if the scales fell off my eyes gradually, until I finally saw what Jesus was saying to his disciples was applicable to me. What also struck me was what Jesus didn't say; the implications are huge. First, he didn't condemn the eunuch, whether he/she was born that way, or was made that way, or chose to become that way. He also did not place any conditions on them with respect to the subjects at hand, marriage and divorce. He also did not list which parings of unions would be acceptable for gender variant persons. Should eunuchs only be paired with other eunuchs? I read somewhere the Hebrew language had five variations for eunuch because only one designation was not enough. For example, they had a word for a female eunuch, and a different word for a male eunuch. In the first case, it was used to designate a mostly female person with some male sexual characteristics, and in the other, a mostly male person with some form of female sexual characteristics. The point Jesus was making was gender and sex are *not* binary in nature, and therefore needed to allow for a broader understanding than simply and only male or female.

Additionally, Jesus' comment *not everyone can accept this* is significant. The statement is similar to when in other places he said, "let him who has ear to hear, hear," or, "eyes to see, see." It is a teaching device, and it is not meant as a declaration of exclusivity for only a few. Rather, it is a challenge to the listeners to *wrap their brain around this* because I want you to *get it!* Jesus wanted to raise their awareness by challenging their small thinking. He wanted to change their paradigm on sexuality.

Finally, this served to temper my expectation that I would enjoy universal acceptance, because not everyone would choose to view things from this much more inclusive perspective.

I find it ironic how the passage I used for years to beat myself into submission was the very one that freed me and gave me permission to be who I am. Unfortunately, the same phrase I used out of context, "the Creator made them male and female," is often quoted by all who oppose lesbian, gay, bisexual and transgender (LGBT) inclusive, doctrines, policies or laws. Listen for this phrase in the sound bites when reporters ask how people feel about same-sex relationships or marriage. It is also ironic how the conservative and right-wing churches and organizations judge and condemn LGBT persons while insisting they love the person, but hate their sin. The volume and temperature of their condemnation, if applied to the issue Jesus was really addressing in the Matthew chapter nineteen discussion, which was divorce and infidelity, would be detrimental to their cause. If they preached against, rejected and judged divorced persons in the same way they preach against, reject and judge LGBT persons, their churches would be empty and so would their bank accounts.

Chapter 27: The Day the Music Stopped

I am not the linguist my older sister Carmen turned out to be, but I am fascinated by the meaning of words. The word "disclose" does not translate into Spanish as directly as the word "disconnect," which in Spanish is *desconectar*. The closest English synonym to "disclose" that has a direct translation might be "divulge," which translates as *divulgar*. In my simple way of thinking, the combination of the prefix "dis," which means to undo, with the word "close," means to un-close, or better still, to open up or to "unhide."

To unhide is a frightening thing to do after fifty-four years, if you discount the first three years of my life when my childhood innocence was still intact. I had never been as terrified or fearful as I was in October of 2007. I had to start unhiding, to open up the door and let all the secrets out. It felt as if I was making a first parachute jump from ten thousand feet: once I stepped off the airplane, there was no turning back; I was committed to going all the way.

After sharing with my pastor I went home to work. I was still tearful as I came in the door, and I felt sick to my stomach—I was emotionally drained. I knew I did not have the emotional stamina to repeat what I had just gone through with all the significant people in my life. If the process of sharing with just one person had been so difficult, I could not imagine doing it ten, twenty, or even thirty times! I was going to need to write it all down. Then I could at least read it to them, instead of trying to explain it every time from memory.

Fortunately, I had a lot of projects to work on, and these relieved my mind of this looming prospect. It was not until Friday afternoon that I was able to get some free time to start *The Letter*. I had been working on a draft for about two hours when a close friend and associate called to find out the status of a job the two of us had been working on. He knew the deadline was not until the following Tuesday, but he just wanted to rest easy over the weekend knowing it was all under control. We talked about the job, and then he asked if I was done for the day. I said yes, and then volunteered I was writing "a sort of biographical thing."

Perhaps that was the wrong thing to say to a professional writer—he immediately wanted to know if he could read it when I finished. I laughed nervously as I answered, "Oh, I don't know, it's kind of personal." As I heard those words come out of my mouth I was immediately upset with myself. Here I was, prolonging the hiding. I corrected myself and said, "Okay, you can read it when I finish it on one condition, you have to read it together with your wife." I should have added, "But pour yourself a stiff drink first."

The following Monday, Duncan called again to discuss a project and asked how my bio was coming. The moment of truth had arrived. I told him it was finished and while we were still on the phone, I attached the file to an email, took a deep breath, and clicked "SEND." Duncan called about ten minutes later, and after expressing his and his wife's unconditional love and support, he admitted he was upset with me. "Why didn't you tell me this before? Me, of all your friends— you knew you could have come to me with this and I would have understood."

I met Duncan around 1977 when he became the new Vice-President of Marketing for the Keg restaurants. We had collaborated on many projects since he started freelancing as a writer. We had attended endless client conferences together, shared long drives and hotel rooms. We had shared countless heart-to-heart conversations about life, death, my brother, our children—but I had never revealed anything about this to him until now. He was truly hurt.

"Every time we had one of those conversations," he said, "I walked away asking myself, 'What is it about Jim that makes him so incredibly sad?'"

Then he remembered how hard he tried to get me to open that door he knew was padlocked tight. I responded that I too remembered all those attempts, and how I always deflected them by changing the subject or making light of the situation. As we hung up the phone he congratulated me for what I was embarking on, and promised to be there for me one hundred percent. He suggested I needed to tell our mutual clients next and several others in our business network as soon as possible. He offered to go through my draft, making some minor edits for me, which I appreciated. His closing comment was "I also promise to say irreverent and politically incorrect things; I will resort to humor, and work hard to put a smile on your face." I hung up the phone for full-blown meltdown number two.

That first version of *The Letter* was full of information about the changes that were going to be taking place in my life some time in the future. The timetable was purposely vague, but suggested these changes would be taking place over several months, if not years. I explained I could not be more specific, because I was still not sure when I was going to share with my aged parents and my sons. I asked this disclosure be kept confidential for now, and to allow me to be the one to share with our mutual friends. *(See Appendix II for current version of the letter.)*

Call it luck, divine inspiration, or woman's intuition, but the next person I disclosed to was the best choice I could have made. She was a woman employed by a computer company that supplied POS (point-of-sale) terminals to the hospitality industry. We met when I worked in-house at the restaurant group. I called her first because I had always felt very safe with her, even though we only had a professional relationship. All I can say is I connected with her and I figured she would be a good gauge for how my other clients might receive the news.

I really should have gone to see her in person, instead I called her and asked if she could talk for about fifteen minutes. Fortunately I called her at a good time. When I told her it was a personal call she excused herself so she could close the door to her office.

She asked, "What's up? Is everything okay?" I told her I would like to read a letter to her if she didn't mind. She gave me the green light and I began reading it.

As soon as I reached the part where I talk about being diagnosed with gender dysphoria, she interrupted, "Stop!"

My heart stopped and I thought, "Oh, no! My life is over."

However, in a very calm and reassuring voice she said, "I know more about this condition than you may know. My brother is a transsexual. And let me tell you something—you don't have anything to worry about with me nor, I suspect, with any of your clients and friends. You are held in high regard and people love you! They're not going to throw you away like garbage. You need to give people the benefit of the doubt that they are not going to judge you or reject you. And let me tell you—you are going to have a much easier transition experience than my brother did."

She went on to explain her brother was a big and tall person and had extra challenges I was not going to face. She asked me to please finish reading the letter and when I finished, she asked about Rachel and our sons. Then we talked for a while. As we were saying good-bye she thanked me for sharing, because she knew it must have been very difficult to pick up the phone to call her. And added I could call her anytime I needed to talk.

It had been just over a week since I shared with my pastor. The phone rang one night, and it was our friend Ann from church whose brother is also transgender. She had heard about my resignation from the worship team but she and her husband were leading the worship that coming Sunday and she wondered if I was really serious about not playing the guitar as well. She was hoping I would be available to play with them, as I always had when it was their turn to lead the worship. I told her I couldn't, that my resignation was not just from leading, but from also being part of the worship team.

She was very concerned for my health, assuming it must be the reason for my resignation. She, too, had seen changes, such as my weight loss, and had wondered if everything was all right. I assured her my health was fine, and suggested that since Rachel and I were hosting the Bible study the following Tuesday night, if she and George could stay afterward, Rachel and I had something we needed to share with them.

I discussed this with Rachel and she requested to see the letter I had written. She wanted the right to edit and or delete anything she was not comfortable with; I agreed. In the end, the changes were minor, we removed a couple of sentences and reworded a few things.

Tuesday night, after the rest of our friends left, the four of us sat around the dining room table facing each other. I unfolded the letter and began to read. When I finished, I could not take my eyes off the paper—I was afraid to look up. Rachel was crying silently and I heard their chairs move as they stood up to come around and hold us.

Ann said "You are going to help me understand my brother so much better."

Then George added, "We love you guys! You have been some of our closest friends and we've been through a lot together. We are with you."

One would think from the level of exhaustion I experienced, the whole world knew by now; when in fact, maybe only eight people had been brought into the loop. This was going to be more difficult than I had ever imagined. I had not even disclosed to any of my family members, and I was bracing myself for all kinds of nasty consequences.

One problem with having a creative and vivid imagination is the tendency to imagine things will turn out worse than they actually do. After I was diagnosed with gender dysphoria, I thought about each of my family members beginning with my sons, followed by my parents and my siblings and, in each case, I imagined the worst-case scenario.

I also imagined the worst responses from close friends and clients. I was prepared for complete rejection, ridicule and contempt if I came out and began making changes. Fortunately, the words of my first client, whose brother was a transsexual, were coming true. Of the few people I had been able to disclose to, not one had said anything that was even close to any of my feared reactions. The complete opposite was true. This quote from Mark Twain really epitomizes my experience: *I've suffered a great many catastrophies in my life. Most of them never happened.*

I wished I could have shouted it from the rooftops and get it over and done with once and for all. The one-by-one approach was definitely going to take time not just in scheduling but in recovering from each encounter! Over the next few weeks I slowed the pace down for two reasons. First, each disclosure left me wiped out, and second, telling my sisters, Carmen and Angela, and their husbands, as well as my brother John and his wife, needed to happen soon. Always worried about how people might feel, I didn't want them to be hurt for not having shared with them while I was telling others.

My pastor and I had kept in close communication, and he wanted to meet with us to discuss an idea he had. He came to our house and asked us if we would consider meeting with a friend of his who was a registered psychologist and marriage counselor. He figured his friend, who had been a pastor in several churches and had taught college and university courses on marriage and family, would be a good person for us to meet so we could enhance our level of communication and work things out. Our pastor had already called his friend, and though it takes months to be worked into his schedule, he agreed to see us within a few days. (In the end, we met with him seven times.)

In late November, one of my restaurant clients opened a new location, and Rachel and I were invited to bring two guests to the grand opening dinner. I decided to ask my sister, Carmen, and her husband. I told them in advance I wanted to share something with them after dinner. Inside the restaurant would not have been appropriate, so I suggested we could sit in their van before they went home. After dinner we climbed in and I read the letter.

My sister's first response was to climb over to the middle bench seat to embrace us and tell us how much she loved us. Her husband reached back and grabbed my hand and squeezed it and said it was going to be okay. After I composed myself and I could speak again, I told them about the response I had received so far, which pleased them. Then we discussed if Mom and Dad needed to know. None of us felt it would be a good idea, but we all agreed we would to have to think really hard about it.

It was a little harder cornering Angela and her very busy husband. We finally managed to get them to come to our house one night, which also happened to be after one of our appointments with the psychologist. We sat at the dining room table as we had done with our friends from church, and I read the letter. Once again, the response was everything I'd hoped for, and not the reaction I imagined and feared.

With Angela and her husband, the concern was when they should tell their daughters about me, my brother-in-law hoping this could be postponed for a very long time. He was worried that since their girls had not even come to terms with their own sexuality this issue could be damaging.

I had thought about this, too, because this would also be an issue for our brother John with his two children. The solution I proposed was to write a personal letter to their girls and to John's son and daughter, which they, the parents, would read to them when they felt it was the appropriate time.

It is important to remember at this time all the big changes were way off in the future—there was no sense of urgency to share with my nieces and nephew. Sharing with my own sons would need to take priority, anyway.

How and when I would begin transition—that was the $64,000 question. I still did not have the confidence to present as a female when I started to disclose to people. My friend Duncan convinced me one day to come visit them as Lisa. His argument was that I needed to start presenting, and what better place than in the safety of close friends. He wouldn't take no for an answer, insisting this was something I had to do.

There was a lot of truth to what he was saying and I concluded he was right about my feeling safe with them. I finally did this one Friday afternoon in early November, 2007. I wore a long-sleeved top with a crew neck, a black skirt, clip-on earrings, and a wig I had recently purchased for $45. I found some low-heeled mules my size at a shoe discount store to complete the outfit.

I will give Duncan and his wife the benefit of the doubt, but I think they were just being polite as they received me that afternoon. As we chatted and had tea, Duncan took some pictures, but I must admit the adrenaline was flowing fast and furious, so the experience was more nerve-racking than enjoyable. My second visit to Duncan would prove even more stressful.

It was the morning of Christmas Eve. Again, Duncan had convinced me to visit them as Lisa for Christmas, and we had a lovely visit. Everything was going well until he said he needed to go to Costco to purchase something. Since I was the card-bearer, the implication was I was to go with him. Costco is about half way between our homes, so the plan was for each of us to drive our own cars and meet in the parking lot. I thought he was crazy for suggesting such an idea, especially on the busiest shopping day of the year. They both assured me no one would know.

"You look fine, dear, better than most of the women who will be there. Just relax, keep your chin up and walk slowly. You'll do fine." Those were his wife's comments as we went out the door.

I remember very little about that trip to Costco—I had tunnel vision from anxiety. I just knew we had to find what he was looking for quickly and make a beeline to the checkout. We were in and out in less than ten minutes—mission accomplished! Back in the parking lot we wished each other Merry Christmas, hugged, and said goodbye.

I don't remember driving home; I know I felt I was going to puke when I came in the door. It was going to be a long time, a *very* long time, before I transitioned, I said to myself. Going out in public was so stressful. Yet it felt right on a different and deeper level: the guilt was gone.

Had Rachel known in advance about my excursion that day, she would have been very upset. Even though the disclosure process was well under way, She would have preferred it if I postponed any public appearance for as long as possible.

There was no denying that the unburdening was making me feel more optimistic. However, I had mixed emotions, because on one hand I wanted to live the rest of my life with integrity and honesty, but, on the other, I was very aware of how the choices I was making were going to impact the person I loved the most, my wife.

At times I felt as if I had defrauded her. My only defense was that I honestly and sincerely believed I was going to be "healed," and would be made "normal." The promises I had made to her were made with all earnestness. Some of the friends I had shared with asked a lot of questions and made comments such as, "Don't you wish you'd been able to come out sooner, when you were younger, so you could have avoided all these years of struggle?" My answer was always "No!" If I had understood my condition and had transitioned at an earlier age I may have avoided the struggle, but I would not have experienced the love from my wife, and the three sons that resulted from our union would not be alive today.

The sad reality is that my best friend has had to pay an enormous price for my changes. As our psychologist aptly put it, the way she felt was as if the train had left the station and she was standing on the platform watching it pick up speed, leaving her behind. For Rachel, it was the death of her husband.

Chapter 28: Hormones

As 2007 came to a close there was a foreboding sense of uncertainty for the new year. There were so many unknowns. At least the wheels were in motion, and though the direction of travel was clear, the road ahead seemed perilous. I knew sooner or later I would have to sit down with my sons, but Rachel and I wanted this to be postponed for as long as possible. If Rachel could have it her way, they would never know the truth about me.

By the middle of January, 2008, the doctor to whom I had been assigned had received all the lab results for my blood tests. I was given my first three-month prescription of the testosterone-blocking medication and the female hormones—this, after reading and signing a lengthy release form that outlined all potential dangers and risks of hormone replacement therapy HRT. From that point on, I would need to undergo blood tests every three months to ensure that my liver and kidneys were not showing any signs of distress.

The feminizing effects of female hormones on the male body are very slow. I did not feel or see any changes for almost three months. The first sign anything was happening was just tenderness in the nipple area. This lasted for a few weeks and then the tenderness spread out as new breast tissue was being formed. I also noticed my skin was softer, especially on my face. I may have been imagining it, but it seemed as if body hair growth had slowed down as well. It's too bad hormones don't stop it from growing altogether. It's also too bad HRT did nothing to improve my receding hairline.

Though the circle of people in my life who knew about the changes to come had grown, the majority still had no idea—especially at church. The changes to my body were not that noticeable during the winter and early spring, since I could layer and hide any noticeable breast growth. I was, however, finding it uncomfortable to jog, and the only solution was to purchase a sports bra. Thanks to a loose-fitting windbreaker I was able to hide the small breast development.

At my appointment in January, when I received my prescription, the doctor asked me if I had attended any support groups. I told him about my contact with the social groups a few years earlier, but said that I had yet to attend a peer support group. He strongly recommended I consider doing so, and told me about the weekly meeting on Thursday nights at the clinic. He explained I did not have to attend presenting as female if I wasn't comfortable, though most who attended did. Alternatively, I could bring my clothes and change in their washroom, and this way I wouldn't have to be out in public. He told me a little bit about the format and hoped I would at least give it a try before my next appointment with him in three months.

I figured what the heck, if I survived Christmas Eve at Costco with Duncan I should be able to drive myself to the clinic and attend my first meeting as my female self, Lisa. For reasons unknown to me the meetings start promptly at five o'clock and end at 7:30 p.m. This meant that I had to leave the house in the middle of rush hour and head downtown on very busy streets. I found the drive considerably more frightening than my drive home from Costco and, when I neared the building, I realized I was going to have to park the car on the street and then navigate a couple of busy sidewalks to reach the front door.

An angel must have been looking out for me just then, because as I turned the corner and came around the front of building, I saw an empty parking space directly in front of the door. I could not believe it. I parked and waited in the car for the sidewalk to be free of pedestrians before I had the nerve to step out of the car and feed the parking meter. Duncan's wife's instructions to hold my chin up high and to walk slowly ran through my head as I put my head down and rushed into the building. What a wimp I was!

I took the elevator to the third floor where the meetings were held, and met a couple of ladies who had just used the facilities to change into their clothes; they were about to enter the meeting room. We said hello and walked together into the large conference room, where all the tables had been gathered in the middle and there were chairs on all four sides. There were enough seats for about forty people. I was surprisingly relaxed as I sat down and hung my coat on the back of the chair.

The moderator entered a couple minutes later and exclaimed, "Oh good, we have some new people tonight. We're just going to wait a few more minutes to give people a chance to arrive, and then we'll get started about 5:15." A few more people trickled in and sat down. The meeting started at the stated time.

After making a few brief welcoming remarks, the moderator then asked who would like to go first. There were about twenty-four of us present, and as I scanned the group closely I determined the majority of the attendees were in their twenties and thirties, a few in their forties, and fewer of us who were fifty or older. I was sitting next to a younger person who identified herself as Elizabeth. She was twenty-seven. Someone raised a hand and volunteered to go first.

The format was to introduce yourself by first name, then share a little bit about yourself. Following that you could ask a question or make a comment, after which the group was welcomed to respond. You could take as little or as much time as needed to say whatever was on your mind.

To cut the story short, I will simply say that I found the meeting very disturbing. As I sat there and listened to person after person share their pain, I realized how fortunate I was in so many ways. A few of the younger transgender persons were sex trade workers because that's all they could do to earn a living. Some, not all, had been rejected by their parents, kicked out of the house at an early age, and had been forced to do whatever they could to survive. A couple of individuals broke my heart, not by what they said, but because I could see how difficult their lives had been just from their physical appearance. Their very big, tall and masculine bodies were always going to sabotage their attempts to blend into society. It made me feel guilty that I had it so much easier by comparison.

However, the hardest thing for me that night was listening to Elizabeth, who was sitting next to me, share her story. She began by explaining she had been on hormones for almost a year, and her surgery would be within six months, if all went well. She had been living in the downtown area for about a year after leaving her home in Chilliwack, a farming community ninety kilometers east of Vancouver.

The previous weekend she had gone home for the first time since she transitioned to come out to her family. It did not go well. She told us about her family and how devout they were in their Christian faith, and how involved in church her parents were. With pain in her voice, she told us how her father had kicked her out of the house and told her never to come back, that she was an abomination to God and was living in sin. She was totally rejected and ostracized by her parents.

You should have heard all the negative, pejorative, snide remarks around the table. "Those church people, they're the worst!" Part of me wanted to slam the table and shout, "It doesn't have to be that way! I'm a Christian, and that has not been my experience!" But I didn't out of cowardice. Another part of me wanted to put my arm around Elizabeth and tell her she was loved by God, and that was all that mattered—but I didn't do that either. I don't know if I was sadder for Elizabeth or sadder for myself for doing nothing.

The meeting ended on time and there was talk about going out for coffee, but I didn't have the stomach for it—I was still reeling from all I had heard. I don't want to give the impression that everything shared that night was a sad story. There were some successes and things to celebrate; I just found myself overwhelmed by the heart-break of the ones who were hurting. I concluded that if this is what happened at every meeting, I would be better off not going. I didn't feel strong enough to invest so much emotional energy into new relationships. I needed encouragement instead of so much sadness.

Chapter 29: The Last Hurdles

As Rachel and I were heading to church a few Sundays after Easter 2008, I was having a conversation with God in my head: "It's been six months since I resigned from worship and no one has come up to me to say they miss my leading or they miss my singing and my guitar playing." And just as quickly as I had that thought, I was confessing to God for allowing my ego to get in the way. "Forgive me Lord, whatever I did in the worship team was not for my glorification—it was to glorify and honor You." Then, just as quickly as I had that thought, I was lamenting to God once again, "But, Lord, it still would have been nice if someone had said something." That was followed by another apology. I went back and forth like this several times. I think the conversation ended with yet another apology.

We got to the church a few minutes early, because Rachel wanted to set up the tables and chairs and all the supplies for her Sunday School class. I made my way up the hallway leading to the front of the sanctuary to listen to the worship team rehearsing the songs we would all be singing that morning. I couldn't go into the sanctuary because ever since I resigned from the worship team, my heart ached and my emotions were too close to the surface whenever I heard worship music. I decided to pace the corridor outside the sanctuary instead of walking in.

Out of a side room came Liz, a woman about my age, who is fluent in Spanish—I believe she was born in Mexico to Mennonite parents. When she saw me, she said, "Oh hi, Jim!" and then in impeccable Spanish said, "I really miss your leading and singing and guitar playing on Sundays. Why aren't you doing it anymore. Were you burned out?"

Her words floored me and I had an instant meltdown. Liz apologized. She wondered if she had said something wrong and recognized she had touched a very soft spot in my heart. Feeling horrible, she came up and gave me a hug; she had no idea what just happened. I said to her I needed to go outside for some fresh air; I also told her she deserved an explanation. The service was not going to start for another fifteen or twenty minutes, so we went for a walk around the block as I told her why I had resigned, and what had been going on. She offered her total support, and told me she loved us unconditionally. She was concerned for Rachel, and wanted to know if there was anything she could do. She was so sweet.

Even now as I recount that little encounter I am overcome with gratitude to God for having answered what, to me, was a very childish and selfish prayer. He didn't hold back; to top it all, it was answered in my mother tongue.

For several weeks I had been praying for direction, for a clear indication of whether or not I should share with my parents. I was trying to weigh my needs to transition against the needs of my parents; I didn't want to ruin their remaining years. In an indirect way I got my answer that morning; I concluded if God was willing to answer such a small prayer, He was capable of answering the big one about my parents.

I had also been thinking about my sons. One day it occurred to me that it would be so very sad if there was something in any of their lives that, out of a fear of rejection from me or of hurting me, they felt they couldn't talk to me about it. How sad it would be if they felt that way! It had also occurred to me that if I felt this way about my own sons, my parents certainly felt the same way about us. They had already demonstrated their amazing unending love for Enrique, and by extension, to all of us. Now, thanks to this simple answer to prayer, I no longer felt afraid to tell them. Instead, I now saw it as an obligation—they needed to know.

My parents lived about thirty kilometers south of Vancouver, within ten minutes of the U.S. border. One of my clients was not far from their house. I had been photographing some food items from their menu, and finished a little sooner than I had expected, shortly after 4 p.m. All afternoon I had been thinking about my parents, rehearsing what I would say to them, and how I would say it in Spanish.

I had real peace in my heart when I called them to say I was a few minutes away from their house, that I had been doing a photo shoot, was just finished packing up, and was hoping to stop by on the way home. Mom and Dad have always loved it when we do things like that. "Of course! How wonderful—do you want to stay for supper?" asked mom. I said no, let's just have coffee together—I didn't want to put her to work.

Dad answered the door when I got there. He had just arrived himself, from a trip to the bank. Mom was in the kitchen getting ready to make coffee, and Dad suggested we have some rum and Coke instead of coffee. I said, "Good idea, Dad, make mine a double." I was energized by the beautiful warm spring afternoon, and was full of anticipation. We sat around the kitchen table and talked about how my day had gone. Mom asked all her usual questions as we sipped our drinks, "How is Rachel? How are the boys?"

After this chitchat, I announced there was something I needed to share with them. Mom's face went ashen, so before I said anything I reassured them my health was fine—I had just had a physical and blood work done, and everything was okay. I added I also wanted to make sure they would not blame anyone, or anything, or themselves—that what I was going to discuss with them was a medical condition. Mom's initial reaction stems from the fact she had been very worried about me because of my weight loss. Every time she saw me, she asked if everything was okay. They had already lost one son to cancer, and she feared the worst every time she saw me.

I began by telling them ever since I was a little boy I had this condition, and only recently had come to understand what it was, and what I could do to overcome it. I recounted some of the childhood memories and events, especially those that were seminal in my thinking and stood out as my vain attempts at understanding what made me feel so different. I asked Dad if he remembered a couple of conversations, and Mom if she remembered some questions I had asked her.

They sort of vaguely remembered some of those things, but there was nothing that stood out in their mind as significant—there were no red flags. As I had suspected, Dad said he just thought I was curious about the facts of life and had written it off to natural curiosity. I went on to explain that through junior and senior high school I had struggled with my image, and that this had continued into my college years. I told them this private struggle is what had brought me to a point of coming to Christ with the hope I would be healed and made normal. At this point in the conversation they still had no idea what I was talking about.

I shared how when I met Rachel I had not allowed myself to think romantically about our relationship, because I was leaving for Canada within a year and didn't want to make saying goodbye harder than it needed to be. They already knew the story of our correspondence and how we had come to realize we were in love.

I told them how much I had hoped being a husband would finally make me complete and normal. But being a husband and then becoming a father, not once but three times, still did not make my condition go away. Then when I was forty I asked to be referred to a psychiatrist and after three sessions with him he offered to refer me to a clinic at Vancouver General Hospital, but I had refused.

I explained how at the time I believed he had helped me enough and felt assured that with Rachel's help and support, I would be able to hang in there. Fast forwarding to 1998—I was now at the point where I needed to go to the clinic and was willing to admit it, I asked to be referred and underwent a very thorough assessment. After about six months, I was diagnosed with a condition known as gender dysphoria.

Dad said he wasn't sure what it meant, but I think Mom had an idea. I explained what it meant, and what the recommended course of action was—with all its ramifications.

At this point, I was holding back the flood of tears I knew was coming. They, too, were teary-eyed, and Mom said, "I can't believe it has taken you this long to tell us. We are so sorry you have been burdened with this and we didn't know."

Dad added, "Yes, I am so proud of you—you are so strong to have carried such a heavy load." Then it was time for the meltdown.

After catching our breath, they asked a lot of questions—how were the boys, did they know? How was Rachel doing? When will you start living as a woman?

Ever since I can remember, I had worried about what my parents' reaction would be if they ever found out about my deep secret. I had feared Dad was going to either slap my face in rage, accuse me of being a "*miriqua*" (queer or fag), or kick me out of the house and tell me I was a disgrace to the family and to never come back. I expected Mom to start pounding her chest like a penitent Catholic and cry that it was all her fault. I had always feared this worst-case scenario, and those fears turned out to be completely unfounded.

My parents not only amazed me with their capacity to accept me, but to do more than that: they loved me.

When I got home I told Rachel what had happened. She couldn't believe I had done something so stupid. She thought I had been reckless and selfish and didn't think it was going to be easy for them. I would have agreed with her a month earlier. Now I knew better, and thanked God for how the day had unfolded and for helping me explain things to my parents—which I did in Spanish.

Having shared with my parents, I felt it was time to share with my sons, and I did. I would have liked to have done it by age, starting with our eldest son, but because he lived out of town that wasn't possible. I tried to schedule a time with our middle son, the one who had some incomplete knowledge about me, but our schedules didn't quite align as I would've liked. Therefore, I shared with the youngest first, who was then twenty-five years old. I read him the letter. As I finished, he reached across the table, grabbed my hands and with tears welling up in his eyes asked me, "Dad, is there anything I can do for you?"

Oh God, those were the most beautiful words I could have heard. "You just did, son, you just did." That was all I could say.

A couple of days later our middle son spent the night at our house—but arrived after I had gone to bed. I found him asleep on the couch the next morning when I came downstairs around 7:00, so I let him sleep a little longer. Then about 9:30 a.m. I started breakfast for the two of us, making enough noise in the kitchen to start waking him up—he is not a morning person.

He was very pleasant throughout our meal, and when we finished I said, "You and I have been needing to talk for a long time. Do you think this might be a good time?"

He said, "Yeah, sure."

I took out a letter I had written for him and read it. As soon as I finished, he stood up, came around the table, and literally lifted me off the floor in his arms. Hugging and kissing me, he apologized for how he had reacted to me almost two years earlier. I apologized for having been so careless and causing him so much anguish. We were finally reconciled and it was all good. It was very good.

Our oldest son and his wife had been doing some minor renovations on their home and we had been coming up on the odd weekend to lend a hand. On more than one occasion I brought the letter I had written to him, but each time Rachel had insisted it was not the right time. But this week began with me sharing with my parents and ended with me sharing with our three sons.

That Sunday we went up to do some work. In return, they invited us to stay for dinner. On a couple of previous visits I had mentioned there was something I needed to share with them one of these days. That night, when I again broached that subject, my son, looking worried, said, "You don't have cancer or something else, do you, Dad?"

I looked to Rachel. She was bracing herself for the moment that had finally come. For the next few minutes I shared with them, and explained what to expect. Their response was also everything I had prayed and hoped for, not what I had feared.

As I think about that week, one thing that stands out in my mind is how I felt when I woke up each morning. Starting with the day after I shared with my parents, I would wake up with this sense of complete and total transparency. I had no more need to hide—everything was out in the open. I could breathe. It was as if I had been released from the dungeon and I could start living, at last. For two weeks I experienced a sense of awe as I awoke each day. It was a new feeling, I finally felt free, and it was wonderful! It took me a while to get used to it.

Chapter 30: Running Into Transition

My next appointment at the clinic was in May, 2008 and I presented as Lisa for the first time. The doctor had seen my photo before, so he didn't notice I wasn't in Jim mode, and it wasn't until I mentioned it to him that he said, "Oh, yes. Congratulations. You look good." If he only knew how rattled I had been as I sat and waited in the crowded clinic, which is really a full-service community health clinic that serves immigrants. That morning, the waiting room was full of families with little children. I did appreciate his compliment, and guess it was worth the anguish.

He reviewed the lab results and said everything looked good, and asked me how I was doing. I told him I had finally shared with my parents and my sons. At the last appointment we talked about my concerns for my parents and how reticent I was to tell them. We talked about how *not telling them* would continue to be an impediment to my transition, unless I was willing to continuously switch back and forth between presenting as male or female.

On this point, we talked about how feasible switching back and forth would be, especially since I was experiencing breast growth, which would be harder to conceal with each passing month. At the time, I was living as Lisa about sixty percent of the time, mostly when I was home alone working in my office.

If I knew in advance a client or a supplier might be dropping by for a meeting, I'd stay in Jim mode. From time to time there were a few surprises from unannounced visits or deliveries, and I had to quickly change out of what I was wearing. Fortunately, I did not wear makeup, so doing a quick switch was possible. I found this going back and forth exhausting in many ways—not physically, but from the mental switch that had to be turned on and off.

The doctor then asked if, since my parents and sons had been brought into the loop, had I made any firm plans for when I would start living as Lisa full-time. I answered I had given it some thought, but just didn't feel quite ready to take that step.

One of the reasons I was holding back was not yet having the courage to share with my Saturday morning running buddy, Franco, with whom I had been jogging every week since 1992. Every Saturday after our run we had a tradition of going out for breakfast, and we had become very close friends. I was worried about his temperament: a second-generation Italian, full of bravado and machismo at the best of times and—I should know—a bit of a chauvinist at the worst. I feared he would not want to run with me ever again. With Franco, it was only a matter of time.

Sooner or later, I knew, I was going to have to give him a copy of *the letter*—and let the chips fall where they may.

The doctor smiled knowingly, and told me he thought everything was going to happen sooner rather than later; he predicted I'd be transitioning very soon. I asked him why he thought so. His experience was when the person finally shared with the most important people in his life, and they have accepted him unconditionally, it changes everything. After that it doesn't matter what anybody else thinks.

That made sense to me. I had reached that conclusion as well after I shared with Mom, Dad and my sons. I did not care what strangers thought and it didn't matter if some friends and clients wouldn't be able to accept me. It was a good appointment.

A few mornings later, I was working at home in Lisa mode when Rachel called to say she was thinking of coming home for lunch, and could I put something together quickly since she only had a half-hour lunch break. We talked about having tuna melts, and agreed she would call as soon as she left the office. I would then go upstairs and put them in the oven so they would be ready the moment she came in the door, as she only works five minutes away from home.

I went upstairs and preheated the oven and prepared the tuna melts and had them ready to bake. As promised, she called to say she was just going out the door. I ran upstairs, put the sandwiches in the hot oven, and went back down to finish an email to a client.

A couple of minutes later I heard the basement door latch being jiggled. Since our latch had been a little sticky, I thought it was Rachel trying to unlock the door. I stood up, rushed to open the door wide open, and said, "Hi!" But instead of my wife, it was my parents! Dad was holding a McDonald's bag and said, "We brought you lunch!"

I was the deer caught in the headlights. I stood there for a few seconds and was finally able to blurt something out. I think I said something like, "Oh, hi, I thought you were Rachel. She's coming for lunch and..." and, "Oh, I have something in the oven! I have to go take it out before it burns. Please come in and close the door behind you." Then I ran upstairs to take the tuna melts out of the oven.

I stood behind the kitchen counter and waited for them to make their way up the stairs. It was too late, I figured—they had seen Lisa, and there was no point running to the bedroom to do the ol' switcheroo.

I stood facing the stairwell as they entered the kitchen. Dad took one look at me and said, "*Como estás de churra!*" which loosely translated means, "You are cute!"

Then Mom said, "Yes, I'm so proud of you! You present very nicely. You have very good taste."

Imagine that. This momentary crisis had lasted all of sixty seconds and it was over. That's all they said—and then we got busy with the business of figuring out where we were going to sit, and how we were going to serve the food they brought. Just then, Rachel came in the front door and stepped into the kitchen. Now she was the deer caught in the headlights; she was speechless. Mom, Dad and I just said hi to her in the most casual way, as if nothing out of the ordinary was taking place.

Poor Rachel. You could have knocked her over with a feather. After she composed herself she said she would feel more comfortable if she could just take her tuna melt back to the office to eat at her desk, adding it was really busy at work.

Rachel went back to work and the three of us sat down and ate our lunch—nothing more was discussed about this little surprise encounter until they were going out the door. Mom reiterated how well I presented, and said she felt at ease knowing I would be all right in public and not draw negative attention to myself. She complimented me once more for my low-key taste in clothing, gave me a kiss and a big hug, and told me she loved me. Mom was so incredibly sweet and sensitive—she used feminine pronouns when addressing me. Then I turned to Dad. He hugged and kissed me and seconded Mom's opinion, and added, "It's like we have a new daughter."

I am so grateful that at their age they could be so amazingly accepting and supportive. I still shake my head in disbelief.

As soon as they drove away—yes, they still drive—I closed the door, and ran to the phone to call my sister, Carmen. "You won't believe what happened just now!" I started. I told her everything, and she started laughing hysterically.

"Oh my," she said, "That was probably the best way for them to meet you as Lisa for the first time. Can you imagine how tense all of you would have been if you had planned to meet?"

She was right.

Getting back to my running buddy Franco. He went to Italy with his parents for a cousin's wedding. They were gone four weeks spanning late June and early July. Before he left, I handed him a sealed envelope with the letter after our breakfast one Saturday. As I had done with Duncan and several other friends whose wives I knew, I asked him to please read it with his wife when they had a few moments away from their children. He looked at me kind of puzzled, but agreed.

All weekend I waited for Franco to call but he never did. I feared the worst. I figured it was over between the two of us. Then, about 8:30 a.m. on Monday morning, Franco's wife Sandra called, and addressed me as Lisa on the telephone. She explained they had just read the letter after breakfast; Franco had just left for work and asked her to please call to let me know he loved me, and this changed nothing. His wife asked if I had any materials or links on the Internet for educational resources, because she wanted to become better informed about what it meant to be a transgender person so that they could know how to be better friends to me and Rachel. She said to call anytime if I needed to talk. This was yet another example of how big people's hearts were towards me and towards Rachel.

During the weeks Franco was away I began jogging as Lisa for the first time. Since I do wear a wig in public, and we were well into summer, I did my running very early in the morning while it was still cool. It seemed to be okay, and I didn't get any strange looks from drivers or people I encountered along my running route. I still had a huge psychological block about running with Franco and going for breakfast afterwards. At least I knew running with a wig was not the impediment I thought it might be.

The first week Franco and I jogged together again I did not run as Lisa—I ran as Jim. We knew he had a lot to share about his trip to Italy, so we agreed to do that over breakfast. Instead, the conversation we had as we jogged was about my plans for transition. He wanted to know if I had made any progress. I told him I was about eighty percent there. He asked when he was going to finally get to jog with Lisa. I said I didn't know, and explained I didn't want to embarrass him or make him feel uncomfortable to be seen in public with me. He rebuffed that notion and asked if I was worried about him or me.

"I think you are worried about yourself," he opined.

Then I pointed out we had been going to the same restaurant for more than ten years and we were regulars there. Wasn't he going to be uncomfortable? He repeated his question, "Are you worried about yourself, or me? Let me ask you something," he continued. "You know the names of some of the staff, but do they know your name—and where you live, and what you do for a living? And the regular customers we always wave hello to: do you know their names, and do they know yours?"

His point was well taken—and yes, I admitted, I was more worried about myself. He then insisted that next Saturday he was jogging with Lisa. That is literally how I started my true transition. From that point on, I never reverted to Jim again.

That Saturday was the first day of the rest of my life, as the saying goes. Jogging on Saturday mornings had been my last hold out.

You are probably wondering how that first run with Franco went. It was anti-climactic. We met at a park half-way between our houses, and when I got out of my car, he gave me the once over, head to toe.

His only comment was, "Hmm, a pony tail. I was wondering how you would have your hair."

Chapter 31: Navigating Uncharted Waters

In retrospect, I had not thought through all the consequences of going full-time. For example, I had not considered all the details, with respect to client meetings. What would I wear? And what would it be like going into a client's office, where I only knew the person I was meeting? Would that person be embarrassed or feel awkward introducing me to his or her colleagues? And should I expect the client to smooth the way for me? Were clients going to feel pressured to do a lot of explaining?

Then there was the issue of church. The way I handled it was by writing a letter to the ministers, telling them I was transitioning full-time, and was no longer going to attend. They had been expecting that. Rachel also decided to stop attending, because she did not want to suddenly become everyone's prayer concern. She would not be able to handle being continually asked how she and I were doing, as well-intentioned people would certainly have done.

There would be other hurdles, such as going through the legal name change, and all that entailed. What the process lacked in complexity, it made up for in lack of speed. I had to undergo a criminal record check with the Royal Canadian Mounted Police; I had to be fingerprinted, and the prints scanned to see if they matched prints from unsolved crimes, for example. So much of it was hurry up, then wait. Then there was a delay caused by the constable who took my fingerprints at the Vancouver Police Department—and then forgot to write his badge number on the card with the prints. The application was put on hold until I could get the constable to sign an affidavit confirming that he was the one who took my prints. So much of it was out of my hands—but that's the way it was.

About eight weeks later I received the official Certificate of Name Change from the Department of Vital Statistics. I was now legally Lisa Salazar. A letter instructed me to now go to all the government agencies I had dealings with—local, provincial and federal— to request my records be updated with the new name. The letter also listed banks, credit card companies, insurance carriers and any entity I had a contractual obligation with. Talk about the domino effect!

First I went to the Driver Services office to update my driver's license. I was given a temporary paper license until the photographic plastic card arrived in the mail. As it happened, on the week I was without a photo driver's license, I had to renew my car insurance. Great. What new hassles was I going to encounter, I wondered. But before I could renew the insurance I had to take my car through Air Care, a provincial requirement to ensure my car's tailpipe emissions were within the allowable limits. Fortunately, the car passed, but not the seal on the gas cap. I was given a rejection notice, and told to bring a new gas cap for testing. If it passed I would be given the authorization to insure the car.

OK, now I was going to finally enter a man's domain, the testosterone den known as an auto parts store. I went twice, not once, because I bought the wrong size. I had to go back to the store and deal face-to-face with a parts-department guy to get the exchange to happen. I had been so happy just going to the aisle with the gas caps and helping myself the first time. Now I had to admit I picked the wrong one for my car. I told the story to a friend who remarked, "That was a very chick thing to do." Gee, thanks!

My car finally passed and I was able to renew my car insurance. I had made a mountain out of a molehill once again, as the lady at the insurance office didn't even bat an eye; she was totally professional. Which brings me to my next observation of things I had not anticipated: being addressed as "Ma'am," being helped with groceries, and having the door held open for me. It was all surreal and my instinct was to say, "Oh, it's quite alright, I can handle it myself."

Angela and her husband were now on the spot. They were going to have to sit down with their daughters and tell them about me. They had planned to do this at their cabin, where they were planning to spend part of the summer. For one reason or another it never happened as they had hoped. They were back in town now, and didn't want to risk the girls finding out accidentally.

The surprising thing to my sister and her husband was how well their daughters took the news when they finally sat the girls down after dinner one night and read my letter to them. Their oldest daughter, who was in twelfth grade at the time, composed the most wonderful letter on behalf of herself and her younger sisters. She mentioned there were a couple of transgender students at their high school, and that they had sessions that dealt with accepting gender diversity as part of their curriculum.

This was yet another example of how we always fear the worst and how unfounded our fears often are.

I got to meet Angela and the girls a couple of days later. They invited me for lunch at their house—we were going to have pizza. What my sister didn't tell me was the pizza was coming from the hot food counter at the Costco near their home, and we were going to go pick it up. She also wanted to drop off six rolls of film for developing—she still owned a film camera. First we went to the food counter to order the pizza since it was going to take ten to fifteen minutes to be ready. Then it was to the film counter. That is when it occurred to me I needed to update my membership card with a new photo and name. I told my sister to go do the film thing, and I would go to the customer service counter.

To my dismay, there was only one attendant, and he looked like a real redneck to me: heavy set and tall. I remembered a little tip from a transgender handout that said, "a smile will disarm a mighty foe," or something like that. I beamed the biggest smile I could make, and walked up to the counter holding my card up to his face.

"I need to update my card," I said, "because this is what I used to look like. I pointed at my face with my other hand. "This is what I look like now."

You should have heard his uproarious laughter, as he said, "Oh heck, yes. We gotta change that real quick! Please come around this side of the counter so I can take a new picture." He was the most pleasant person I could have imagined. He was so polite when he asked what name I wanted to use, and if I needed to change any other details. It was a great experience and ironically a lesson in the importance of not prejudging people by their looks.

Old habits are hard to break. I don't want to sound as if I am making excuses for myself; I used prejudice as a defense mechanism all my life in order to survive. But, most often, I was judging myself.

Transitioning that July, 2008 did have one unfortunate consequence: I would not be able to attend my 40th high school reunion as I had intended. Back in January, I had indicated to the organizers of the reunion that I would be coming. It was great that from their emails I had been able to glean some email addresses of old classmates, some of whom I had not communicated with since we graduated from high school in 1968. I had finally re-connected with them, and we were all excited about the reunion in September.

In early August I sent an email to this small group of friends and to the organizers expressing my regrets that I would not be able to attend. Within a few days I received several emails, pleading with me to rearrange my schedule and not to miss this chance of a lifetime to be with people I may never see again. I had no choice but to write these individuals to explain the reason, and asked them to please keep it confidential. Additionally, I did not want to hijack the evening by being the center of attention even if it was for only five minutes.

Perhaps one of the most wonderful things that has come out of all this is how people have responded to my disclosure. I've talked about my meltdowns in this book, and there have been many. Mostly there has been tears of joy and gratitude for the overwhelming flood of love and support. I have been impressed by people's eloquence— expressing their hearts using the simplest of words to say the most profound things. I have collected all these emails, and deeply treasure them. I don't read them very often because I know that I will not have enough Kleenex in the house for the experience.

When I was diagnosed in 1998, and was briefed on what choices were available to me and explained the "road map" to womanhood, there were two items that made it completely impossible to contemplate. One was that I would have to start living as a woman right away. The other was if and when I had the surgery, Rachel and I would not be able to remain legally married. We would need to be divorced. These two requirements were, to me, deal breakers.

In 2007, when I returned to the Clinic, one of the first things I said to my doctor was though I needed help I was going to have an issue with those conditions. However, I discovered a lot had changed in nine years; the protocols had been relaxed. The Clinic agreed with my reservations, and would work with me at my own speed. I also stated I did not want to undergo gender reassignment surgery (GRS), since I was married, in a loving relationship, monogamous, and had no desire to have intimate sexual relations with a man. My point was that I had no need for a vagina.

With respect to the divorce requirement, this had become a moot point since in 2005 Canada became the fourth country in the world, and the first country in the Americas, to legalize same-sex marriage nationwide. I would not be forced by law to divorce Rachel if I ever decided to have the GRS.

As to transition, from that first meeting I explained concern for my parents and my reticence to disclose to them. I was resigned to the fact as long as they were alive I would not be able to transition. My doctor was okay with that, too.

What was different now was the Trans Health Services group were taking patients' needs into consideration and allowing the protocol to be tailored to accommodate them as best they could. This was very different compared to how it was before, when the patient had to follow the protocol or not be helped at all.

I have shared how much it pains me to see how my choices have impacted my best friend, Rachel. Recently, in a conversation with my dad, he commented what I was doing to Rachel was too hurtful. He asked why I couldn't say to myself that I had endured my condition for fifty-eight years, and that I might as well stay unchanged for however many years I may have left to live and return to being Jim for her. "Yeah, right! If it was only that easy." I thought to myself.

I asked him if he would say the same thing to me if what I had was another "congenital" or lifelong medical condition for which there was now a procedure that could improve the quality of my life. Should I not have such a procedure performed on me, or should I say to myself that I've lived with it this long and I might as well take it with me to the grave.

"That's different," he said.

"How so?" I asked. But his point was well taken. My decision has impacted Rachel's self-image in a fundamental way, since it defines her as someone radically different than my wife. How I wish I could have been strong, to stay the course and remain as Jim for Rachel.

When friends have remarked they are happy for me because I am finally doing something I've wanted to do all my life, I feel compelled to correct them and point out this is the last thing I wanted to do. When others say I am courageous, I correct them for that, too. I tell them I was desperate. There is nothing admirable about what I did. I see it simply as basic survival.

I deal in pictures—I make my living doing visual stuff—so it was no great surprise that an image came to mind one day as I was trying to explain to someone how I saw my life: I remembered unraveling a large ball of heavy string I found when I was a child. I pulled on the end that was poking out of the center and started pulling on it. I kept this up until the ball lost its critical mass and what was left collapsed and was formless. Until that very moment, the outside shape was intact and one would not have known that its core was slowly disappearing by just looking at it. That was me, and that was my life. I was unraveling from the inside, but no one was the wiser. I knew my "critical mass" would soon be gone and I would collapse into an unrecognizable heap. I didn't want that to happen to me for Rachel's sake. I didn't want that to happen for our sons' and the rest of my family's sakes, either.

I knew it was not healthy to dwell on death all the time and to think that death would solve my gender problem. But why hadn't God taken me on any one of the many times I had close calls, where I've lucked out. "Why didn't you take me then?" I have asked God so many times. To simply say my time had not yet come is a cop out. Why hasn't it been my time? Why am I still around?

Don't get me wrong: I love life as much as the next person, and from that human point of view, I know there is a lot I would miss if I were gone. I am not talking about missing material things; I'm talking about things of the heart. I would miss people—my friends and extended family, my sons, but most of all my wife. Despite the fact I have often thought death would solve so many problems, I am grateful I am still around, even if I have to learn to live in a whole new way. As I said to the man at Costco, "That is what I used to look like; this is what I look like now."

The challenges will continue—how Rachel and I will be able to navigate these waters is still a big question mark. In her own words, we are no longer husband and wife. For now we remain legally married and dwell together under the same roof, but live very separate live and independent lives. The exception is during family events.

I have a transsexual friend who is basically one year ahead of me in the process. I was encouraged by the fact that she was still with her spouse after the surgery and it looked as if their marriage was going to endure. I was sad to learn recently it doesn't look like it will survive after all.

Though we live in a city, province, and country that are fairly enlightened to transgender issues, there is still a stigma for some. An uneasiness remains but is seldom talked about—it is the elephant in the room. I am that elephant and I know it. It is conjecture on my part, but I believe so many transsexual marriages fail because the spouse is incapable of withstanding this insidious silence.

Rachel once asked me how I would feel if the tables were turned, if she came to me wanting to have her breasts removed, to grow a beard and become a man: would I still want her if "she" was a "he?" My honest answer was that I could not imagine how I would feel. Therefore my honest admission is that I do not know the extent of her pain, or what she has had to endure. And she is also not able to live my pain. The two are different but they are both very real. One is not easier than the other.

A client of mine recently made a comment in reference to some turns of events that have impacted their business negatively. They were facing large losses and possible bankruptcy. She commented, "business is business" and one must be prepared to walk away from it and not let it consume you. That can't be said about marriage—certainly not my marriage.

There will be other challenges, which are part of the deal. It's taken me a while to fully appreciate some of these because I have been living, until recently, as a male. For example, as a woman I can no longer go for jogs late at night like I used to do. In the summer, I had actually gone on five-mile runs at midnight. Not anymore.

As a transgender person there are other risks I will face, and have already experienced. In the summer of 2009, I had dinner with my friend Duncan, his wife and a mutual friend at a new restaurant that had just opened downtown. With the exception of the friend, the rest of us arrived on one of the two rapid transit trains that feed into downtown Vancouver. Duncan and his wife arrived on the new Canada Line, which connects downtown Vancouver to the international airport. When it was time to go home, I decided to go with them part of the way and get off at the 49th Avenue station—one of the stops along the way—from which I could take a bus, travelling east to my house. The trip would be slightly longer than if I returned on the other train, which was a more direct route. But trying out the new train with some friends was too irresistible.

When we boarded the train, it was already two thirds full and there were only a few empty seats. Duncan's wife sat down in the first seat she saw by the doors. Duncan and I stood next to her holding on to the pole for support. Across the aisle in front of the other set of doors there was a man in his late twenties holding onto the pole on his side of the train. Shortly after the train started moving through the tunnel the guy started muttering something that I couldn't make out.

After the train left the next station he got a little louder and I glanced over to see what was going on and he was making some pretty menacing gestures in my direction, so I ignored him. I concluded he might have Tourette's syndrome and leaned forward and made a comment to that effect to Duncan and his wife. But she looked at me and said, "Oh, no, dear, he's talking about you."

I was totally freaked out and terrified, but I couldn't let it show. I tried to stay as calm as I possibly could by ignoring his comments, which I could barely make out above the noise of the train and all the conversations. I started thinking about my options, wondering what I should do. Should I stay on the train and go all the way with Duncan and his wife? I could then take a train back to 49th Avenue and catch a later bus to go home.

To my relief, he got off at the station before mine. I kept my eye on him to make sure he remained on the platform until the train pulled away. I got out at my station but now I was rattled, so I left the train with a group of foreign ESL students and stayed close to them until we reached the bus stop at street level. When the bus finally arrived, passengers were packed like sardines; it was standing room only. My heart still racing from my previous incident, I took a deep breath, boarded the bus, and crossed my fingers for everything would be okay the rest of the way home.

With so many people on board and the bus making every stop along the way, it was going to be a long ride. After about six stops more people boarded, among them a tall male in his sixties. He looked like he'd had a few too many and was a bit wobbly on his feet. To my dismay he looked right at me, smiled broadly and came and stood next to me. The next thing I knew he was stroking the bare skin of my arm with his hand. I pulled it away and gave him a stern look. He continued grinning at me.

The woman sitting next to where I was standing got up from her seat a few stops later. I sat down. Now the man was standing over me. I ignored him until the young fellow in the window seat excused himself to exit the bus. I had no choice but to move into the vacated window seat, knowing the man would most likely sit next to me—and he did. Now I was trapped. He tried to put his arm around me but I gave him a dirty look and he withdrew his arm. This little scene came to an abrupt end when he suddenly jumped to his feet when the bus reached his stop. He wobbled off the bus and he was gone.

I know I've gone into a lot of detail about this incident—but it was a jolt to my composure. After one year of living as a transgender female I went from being an object of scorn to an object of lust in less than fifteen minutes. I felt vulnerable for the first time, as a transgender person and as a woman.

I shared my experience that night with Rachel, and she was not surprised by either of the two incidents. She told me, in no uncertain terms, what I should have done and warned me as to what I should do in the future if I find myself in similar situations. I felt like a little schoolgirl being admonished and lectured on how to be street safe.

Chapter 32: The Change

The first twelve months of living full-time are called "the real life test." It is a significant milestone on the transsexual road map, because after one year of living full time and surviving, one is eligible for gender reassignment surgery (GRS). That is, of course, if you pass the psychological assessment.

As I mentioned earlier, originally I did not plan to have the surgery. What tipped the scale in favor of it was a conversation I had with my doctor at the clinic. Unfortunately, some of my blood tests had given the clinic some concern. Both my kidneys and liver had shown signs of distress, and the doctors had even considered taking me off the medications if the next test showed similar results. However, if I were to have the surgery, I would be able to go off most medications. If I didn't, then I would need to continue taking them for the rest of my life if I still wanted to suppress testosterone, which would keep me at risk for all kinds of complications. That was reason number one for reconsidering GRS.

Reason number two had to do with the legal and safety aspects of living as a woman but still being identified as male in all of my official documents, including passport and driver's license. If I planned to travel, the incongruity between how I presented and my stated gender could potentially cause some problems, depending on the jurisdiction. There would always be the risk of being delayed, humiliated or worse, if some official were to make a case out of it.

The third reason was a moot point for me—validation. Some transsexuals view the surgery as the ultimate validation of who they are, and this is all the reason they need. For others, it is crucial for them to undergo GRS so they can enjoy heterosexual intercourse and function sexually as a woman. Neither of these was of any consequence or significance to me. I didn't need the surgery for validation, and the last thing I wanted to do was make love to a man, since I have never been attracted to men.

I chose to request surgery on the medical and legal/safety issues alone. For my one-year anniversary appointment at the clinic I brought letters from individuals who could vouch that I had been living full-time for one year. I asked a couple of clients and a couple of friends for such letters, since letters from family members were not accepted. My doctor then submitted the letters, along with his report and a copy of my file to the provincial Trans Health Services office in Victoria, the provincial capital. He told me this office would contact me in about three months to schedule me for the psychological assessment.

In September, I got a call from the provincial office requesting my email address so I could be notified about when and where the assessment would take place; they suggested it would be sometime in October. The following week, however, I was called again, because they had a cancellation and I could be seen sooner. The assessment, done by two of the Trans Health psychiatrists, lasted one hour; I was approved for surgery. Then I had to wait another three months for the Authorization for Surgery letter from the Ministry of Health. With that letter in hand, I could call the hospital in Montreal to book a date for the GRS. For now, the Province of British Columbia farms out the surgery to the clinic of Dr. Pierre Brassard, a world-renowned GRS specialist. Travel and extended care for recovery are the patient's responsibility.

The Authorization letter arrived the week before Christmas, so I called the hospital to book a date; the earliest would be May 17, 2010—a five-month wait. I wanted to think about whether the other dates might work best for me, but since the hospital was closed for two weeks over Christmas and New Year's I was asked to call back in

January. I chose the first date they had given me, May 17th—but, once again, there had been a cancellation. March 30th was now available so I went for it.

Friends have wondered if I would be attracted to men, and if I would consider that possibility in the event that my marriage does not survive. My instant and emphatic answer has always been no, I do not wish to have any intimate relation with a male. I am not curious or remotely interested in such a thing, and never have been. The surgery does not change one's sexual orientation. If I were not monogamous and celibate, I would be open to an intimate relationship with a female—I suppose, technically, that would make me lesbian. And that's an issue for Rachel: she is one hundred percent heterosexual.

The best explanation I have heard about this complicated multi-level issue of gender, sex and orientation, was by Dr. Cameron Bowman of the University of British Columbia, the only gender surgery specialist in our province. In an interview on a local cable community program, the interviewer asked the question if all transsexuals were attracted to the members of their original sex, now their opposite sex. He explained the need to take each of these three areas and discuss and understand them separately.

Gender, he said, is how we identify ourselves—it is the brain's imprint. We either identify as male or female, but there are some who identify as neither—they are asexual; others identify as a combination of both; and yet others as more of one than the other, but not one *or* the other.

He described *Sex* as the body's biological, physical characteristics—the plumbing. Again, most have either fully developed male or female "plumbing," but there are a few who have ambiguous sexual characteristics and cannot be categorized as either male nor female— they are intersex.

Finally, there is sexual *orientation*. Again, most people are attracted only to the opposite and never to their own sex. However, there are some who can go either way, or are only attracted to their own sex.

What complicates things is that each of these layers is a spectrum and when you superimpose all three, you have an endless set of possible combinations.

The majority of people have a gender imprint that matches their body and they never question or wonder what they are. If you are one of these, consider yourself fortunate. For me and for many like me this has not been the case. And it goes both ways. There are women who identify as male and men who identify as female, others who identify as both male and female; and yet others who identify as more of one, but not totally. It is not an issue of being right or wrong. We cannot and should not be so literal as to say, "You have a man's body, therefore, you are male."

If you don't struggle with your gender imprint, at least give those who do the benefit of the doubt, and be open to the amazing diversity in our human family. None of us gets to choose and that should keep us all humble, compassionate, and inclusive.

In Chapter 26, I talked about how I came to a new understanding of Jesus' comments about eunuchs. That was a pivotal point in my life, because it was then I was finally able to reconcile faith with what the doctors had told me. It was only after I saw God was not going to judge me for the choices I needed to make, and that my faith was not at odds with what I was, that I finally felt I had permission to proceed.

I must admit, however, there was a touch of doubt that lingered in my mind. Was I fooling myself, and only seeing this issue from a selfish point of view? Any doubt I may have had evaporated when I realized there was corroborating evidence in the Bible. I now believe the disciples did come into a new understanding of human sexuality, (as well as marriage—the high calling of the committed, intimate relationship between two persons) as a result of Jesus' teaching discussed earlier. The evidence is in St. Luke's account in the Book of Acts, about Philip's encounter with the Ethiopian eunuch. Luke tells it like this:

But an angel of the Lord spoke to Philip saying, "Get up and go south to the road that descends from Jerusalem to Gaza." So he got up and went; and there was an Ethiopian eunuch, a court official of Candace, queen of the Ethiopians, who was in charge of all her treasure; and he had come to Jerusalem to worship, and he was returning and sitting in his chariot, and was reading the prophet Isaiah. Then the Spirit said to Philip, "Go up and join this chariot." Philip ran up and heard him reading Isaiah the prophet, and said, "Do you understand what you are reading?" And he said, "Well, how could I, unless someone guides me?" And he invited Philip to come up and sit with him. Now the passage of Scripture which he was reading was this:

"HE WAS LED AS A SHEEP TO SLAUGHTER;
AND AS A LAMB BEFORE ITS SHEARER IS SILENT,
SO HE DOES NOT OPEN HIS MOUTH.
"IN HUMILIATION HIS JUDGMENT WAS TAKEN AWAY;
WHO WILL RELATE HIS GENERATION?
FOR HIS LIFE IS REMOVED FROM THE EARTH."

The eunuch answered Philip and said, "Please tell me, of whom does the prophet say this? Of himself or of someone else?" Then Philip opened his mouth, and beginning from this Scripture he preached Jesus to him. As they went along the road they came to some water; and the eunuch said, "Look! Water! What prevents me from being baptized?" And Philip said, "If you believe with all your heart, you may." And he answered and said, "I believe that Jesus Christ is the Son of God." And he ordered the chariot to stop; and they both went down into the water, Philip as well as the eunuch, and he baptized him. When they came up out of the water, the Spirit of the Lord snatched Philip

*away; and the eunuch no longer saw him, but went on his way rejoic-
ing.*

There are so many lessons we can unpack from this story. For example, the Ethiopian eunuch's devotion to Judaism had compelled him to make the long, treacherous, and dangerous journey to Jerusalem from Ethiopia to celebrate the Jewish feast of the Passover. He did this even though, as a eunuch, he was unable to enter the Temple grounds to fully participate in the feast, since, as was the custom at the time, eunuchs were considered ceremoniously unclean. He could therefore only stand on the sidelines and watch; he was an excluded person, through no fault of his own.

I appreciate you may not hold the same beliefs as me about Jesus, and I am not sharing all of this with you to convince you one way or another. I simply want you to understand that it was important for me to work these things out. As I said earlier, I needed to reconcile what I was inside with my faith. The narrow focus and very simplistic views I had held is what made it so difficult for me to accept what I was. This was the tension and the battleground, and nothing made sense for most of my life.

As a believer and follower of Jesus, what touches me about this story is this is one of the first acts by one of the apostles, and more significantly, it is the act of including sexually and anatomically "other" persons. Additionally, for this to be one of the first "church" events is evidence things were going to be different from the very start. It declared that none would be excluded for being "different." That Philip did not hesitate to reach out and affirm this sexually-other person as a believer is an equally monumental lesson. I suspect Philip must have been just as surprised as the eunuch by this amazing encounter.

When the eunuch asked Philip if he shouldn't be baptized, he wasn't saying, "Hey, I want to start out right by following the new rules." Instead, the question was packed with so much more importance. It was as if he was saying, "Though I have been a devout Jew all my life and have done everything that is expected and demanded of me, even coming to Jerusalem to celebrate the Passover, I have not been a full participant. As an other-sex person, I have had to stand on the sidelines. Will this also be the case now, or can I be a full participant as an equal?"

Humor me a little bit longer, and just imagine how the eunuch must have felt to no longer be marginalized and excluded. He was now an equal. How could there be no rejoicing? That, in essence, is how I finally feel after almost six decades. I finally accept myself as a woman, and though there is still a long road ahead and it won't always be smooth travelling, I am finally able to rejoice in who I am.

With that said, I must say good-bye; it's time to finish packing the suitcases. My flight is tomorrow morning and the surgery is in a couple of days. My surgeon is waiting!

As the day of my surgery approached, I gave myself the self-imposed deadline to finish the book on the eve of my departure for Montreal and to end it with "My surgeon is waiting!" But when my friend and instigator in this book writing project read the first draft, she protested that I could not end the book with that sentence since this would leave too many unanswered questions in the mind of the reader. She was right. I thank Jan Williams for her valuable suggestion to add an epilogue and the appendices that follow. L.S.

Chapter 33: An Epilogue

The flight from Vancouver to Montreal via Calgary was uneventful for the seasoned crew of the *WestJet* 737 that day. But in the mind and reality of a transgender person on her way to surgery, this trip was the final destination.

Three months earlier, when all the final arrangements for gender reassignment surgery were made, the date seemed so far away. I sent all my clients an email telling them I would be away for three to four weeks beginning the last week in March. I did not elaborate why, but they all knew. Congratulatory replies started coming in within minutes.

As the date drew closer, the two questions I was asked most often were, "Are you excited?" and "Are you nervous?" The fact was I was neither. What I felt was relief that I would no longer be in limbo, straddling the gender divide.

Six weeks before the surgery I had to have blood work and an electrocardiogram, with the results being sent to Dr. Brassard in Montreal. Three weeks later I stopped taking all medications as instructed, to ensure my body would be free of anything that might prevent a quick recovery.

My intention was to travel to Montreal on my own, which is what the majority of Dr. Brassard's patients do. My two sisters were not happy that I was going to be alone, and decided to do a tag team. One would come for the first days, and the other would take her place a few days later. In the end, only Carmen made the trip, since her work schedule allowed her more flexibility. She arrived in Montreal the day of my surgery, Tuesday, March 30. I arrived in Montreal on Sunday, the twenty-eighth, in the early evening. A limousine picked me up at the airport and took me to the "residence of convalescence" next door to the small private hospital.

Dinner was on the table when I walked in. I was welcomed by the nurse on duty, and introduced to some of the other patients before I was escorted to my room, which I shared with a young woman from Ottawa. Her surgery had been earlier that week, and she was resting. I placed my bags on my side of the room and went back downstairs to eat dinner.

I was the last patient to arrive for the upcoming week's surgeries. The hospital and residence were going to be closed for one week to give the doctors, nurses and staff some well-deserved time off.

In all, there were seven of us when I arrived—four Canadians and three Americans. I was the oldest at fifty-nine; the youngest was twenty-four years old. As I mentioned, three of us were scheduled for surgery; the others were recovering from theirs. It was very moving to be among them all. Our stories were so similar, yet so radically different and unique.

I met Dr. Brassard on Monday afternoon, and we discussed the surgery. He answered all of my questions. I cannot say enough about him and his staff; my experience was very positive, to say the least. The most surprising thing to me was how calm I was before the surgery. I say this because I have always been squeamish when it comes to blood. I can't even look at myself getting poked with needles—and I have I been poked with many needles in the last two years.

I brought my laptop to Montreal so I could keep in touch with family and friends, thanks to *Skype* and email. How great that was to talk to my parents and to several friends for free. Many friends had asked me to let them know how I was doing so I sent updates whenever it was feasible. *(See Appendix I)*

Carmen was so sweet, not only to me, but to the other individuals. I am so grateful she came after all. I was the only one with a family member who came to be by their side. My heart went out to the younger ones, so alone and far from home at such an important moment in their lives. What was beautiful to see and experience was how everyone offered love and support to each other. The staff at the hospital and at the residence was also amazing in this way—they made us feel completely safe and cared for, especially since we all seemed to be highly emotional.

In all, I spent two and a half days in the hospital after the surgery, and one week at the residence recovering. I came back to Vancouver after eleven days, on April 8. I must admit it was very difficult to leave Montreal and, even today as I write this, four weeks after my surgery, I miss the friends I made during my brief stay there.

In one of my updates I mention time is so strange—how it seemed to be crawling slowly the first few days after the surgery—and then how it seemed to speed by in a blur. It seems like my surgery was only yesterday but then it feels like it was so long ago. Isn't it strange, this thing called time?

Some final thoughts: I have used the journey metaphor ad nauseum, but that is what life is, a journey. We can choose to embrace our fellow sojourners with respect, compassion, and dignity, and go on our way rejoicing together—or we can choose to let our differences isolate and insulate us from each other. What an amazing choice! We can resort to secrecy and hiding, or we can walk and live transparently. That's the lesson I have learned. I am not journeying alone and I am grateful to be alive and grateful for who I am.

We live in a world with a deep need of repair, full of people born into or with many difficulties they never chose for themselves. It behooves us, then, not to judge and condemn, but to be radically involved in building up, rather than tearing each other down—and to do it out of love and respect for the person. I will end with these lovely verses from Micah 6:6-7: *He has shown you, O mortal, what is good. And what does the LORD require of you? To act justly and to love mercy and to walk humbly with your God.*

The Last Word:

This book must end with a tribute to Rachel, who has had to pay a very big price due to the choices I needed to make. As a friend put it, her story deserves to be told, too—how she has dealt with the hurt, shock, loneliness, love of Jim, loss of Jim, living with Lisa, etc. She is truly an admirable person, but she is also a very private person with an equally strong and private faith. She deserves and has all my love and respect. As we now go our separate ways, I wish her peace.

Appendix I: Bed Posts

Monday, 29 March 2010 — Montreal

Good morning all,

It's going to take me a few days to adjust to the three-hour difference. I see it is only 7:00 AM in Vancouver. Just wanted to say that I'm all settled in at the hospital. Surgery is tomorrow in the morning. I will be out of touch for the next three days but will try to give you an update as soon as I can. There are three others from the lower mainland: one from New York, one from Florida and one from California. I have the distinct privilege of being the oldest present. It is a private hospital and the "residence" is just like a bed and breakfast, very comfortable and nicely appointed.

The weather today in Montreal looks like Vancouver—rainy. I will be prepped for surgery around 4:00 P.M. and then will be fasting from that point on.

How am I doing? The best way to describe it is that I feel as if I'm coasting to the finish line, the hard part of the race is behind me. It is the feeling of relief. It surprises me that I am not nervous or anxious. I figured I would be by now, but I am not. I credit this to the way all of you have allowed me to continue this journey with your friendship and support. Thanks!

Drop me a line when you get a chance. I may not be able to answer you personally and may have to rely on an open letter like this to email to all of you on my list.

Bye for now.

Lisa

Wednesday, 31 March 2010 — Montreal

Good morning all.

I took out my laptop about an hour after I got a shot of morphine. I wanted to write an update and save it for sending later. (The Wi-Fi connection does not work inside the hospital; it is only available in the "bed and breakfast") So I composed this witty and funny update saying among other things, how wonderful it was to have the anesthesiologist telling me the anesthesia IV was in, that I'd feel sleepy very fast and a second later, hearing a nurse say to me: "Lisa, Lisa, you are in the recovery room and we'll be taking you down to your room in a couple of hours—your surgery was perfect. Congratulations!"

I then saved the email and when I reached to close the laptop, I couldn't feel it... It wasn't there! I had been hallucinating the whole time. So it is now about eight hours later and I'm writing this email for real this time. I think. I will now save it for sending when I return to the recovery house next door on Thursday night.
Lisa

PS: I think this is a more interesting email than the holodeck version anyway. Just noticed a very weak Wi-Fi signal, will try to send now.

Thursday, 1 April 2010 — Montreal

Good morning all.

April Fool's Day! Hmm, I will resist the temptation to play a joke.

I left the hospital's primary care unit and am back in the residence for the week of recovery. I am doing much better than I had expected. The only unpleasant and unexpected thing happened last night: I rolled over in my sleep and pushed the plastic end of the draining tub in further. I woke up with a jolt; it felt like I had been stabbed in the gut. After I rolled back on my back and repositioned the tube, it helped but for the next few hours it felt like I had a pencil stuck in me. Fortu-

nately, the tube came out this morning.

If that is the worse part of all of this, I will be a very happy camper.

For the next few days, it is just rest that is on the agenda. I brought a good book; the only problem is that I feel like I have A.D.D. and nothing holds my interest for more than a few minutes. Even this email is the result of two sessions. Heck, I'm bored already. But I do love you all.

Until later.

Lisa

Saturday, 3 April 2010 — Montreal

Good morning!

I was able to take my first post-op shower this morning after breakfast! When the others who were ahead of me talked about their first shower, I thought to myself, "What's the big deal, it's only a shower?" Well, now I know why they were so elated... the truth being that you can only shower once all the gauze padding and dressings—which are sutured on—have been removed and one is finally au naturel! Oh, yes! Now I see why it is cause for celebration! (SORRY to be so specific. I hope I didn't put any disturbing images in your head.)

Today, the weather in Montreal is sunny and will be in the low 20s Celsius (70s Fahrenheit). I've been waking up at 6:00 AM just about every day so I hope to be up for Easter Sunday sunrise tomorrow morning to celebrate Life in earnest. I hope it won't be cloudy because the sunrise is really pretty through my bedroom windows.

I forgot to pack my small digital camera. I've been using my cell phone to take photos but I haven't got the mental stamina to set up the Bluetooth connection between it and my laptop to download the photos. I'll leave it for a couple of days.

Funny things, those endorphins, even though I won't be in any shape to run for a few weeks, all I have to do is see a jogger run by in the park across the street and I get the craving.

I also have a new craving—shopping! I'm told that comes with the territory. It will have to wait. Attention span is much better. That was weird a few days ago when I could not stay focused on anything for very long. It's still not what I would call all there yet. "Squirrel!"
Lisa

Tuesday, 6 April 2010 — Montreal

It's getting better all the time. The end of the long weekend and life will return to its usual volume in the morning.

It was pretty quiet around here the last three days and the only time I got to see the two other patients was at meal times. I think I mentioned that there are only three of us here for now. One of the other two is leaving on Wednesday and the third one leaves on Thursday with me; she is from California. The residence and the hospital will then be closed for 7 days to give all the doctors and nurses some time off. The intake of new patients will resume on the following Thursday.

Carmen, my older sister, came to Montreal the day before my surgery to be with me. She goes back to Vancouver on Wednesday. I think the two of us were a little optimistic to think that we would be able to tour the city together. I need to follow a pretty strict regimen post-op stuff that repeats itself three times a day; there is no time to be a tourist. Nevertheless, I am so grateful that she came even though she had the tour of Montreal by herself. All the other girls who are here came alone. My heart goes out to them, especially for the girl from California, she is only 24 years old. So young in so many ways, but she is a very sweet person.

Thank you for all your emails. I look forward to checking my computer whenever I get a chance. It's been great to stay connected.

I see it is only 1:45 P.M. on the West Coast. I just woke up and took a warm shower. It felt so good—no more tubes and bandages to worry about. I'm going to sneak down for a cup of cranberry tea.

In closing, one of the best medicines has been a 3-minute video on YouTube called Upular. It always puts a smile on my face. Check it out!

Lisa

Thursday, 8 April 2010 — Montreal

Two hours left to go before the limo comes to the residence to drive me to the airport. If this were a regular Bed & Breakfast, I would certainly be singing its praises and telling you all to stay here if you ever visit Montreal, but I have a hunch that none of you will be putting it on your list of things to do.

Though it seemed like time was standing still on the first few days after the surgery, looking at it from this end, time has flown by. It's the weird thing about time—it's all so relative.

I am the last to leave; the girl from California was picked up at 11:30 AM so I've had the place to myself. Wow, if walls could talk. It is pretty emotional sitting here in the living room as I leaf through the "Guest Book," so many stories like mine but uniquely different in so many ways. The head nurse tells me the waiting list keeps getting longer, that all we are seeing is the tip of the iceberg. Who would have thought?!

Thanks again for your emails. I will be lying low for at least the next 10 days but don't hesitate to email, call or visit if you are passing through South Vancouver.

Lisa

Appendix II: The Letter

First drafted in October 2007, it has gone through several revisions to keep it current and up to date with the changes in my life. Last revised March 30, 2010.

To my friends —

I'll begin by telling you that I'm not a big risk taker, for fear of my worst fears becoming reality. I have feared rejection, ridicule, humiliation, losing friends, being the object of mockery, not blending in, being different, hurting or embarrassing loved ones, and as a self-employed person, I have feared losing clients.

I need to take the risk of sharing something about myself with you—secrecy is no longer an option and I have come to realize that disclosing to you is the only way our relationship can continue, if it is to have integrity.

About ten years ago, after a lifetime of guilt and confusion, I was diagnosed as having gender dysphoria at Vancouver General Hospital's Gender Clinic—a condition commonly referred to as being a transgender person, or a transsexual. This diagnosis was simultaneously a blessing and a curse. It was a blessing because it provided an explanation of my past and a signal of hope for something that might end the guilt, confusion and shame, but it was a curse because the options and choices offered to me not only had a hefty personal price tag, they also confirmed that there were no magic cures that could make me "normal." While I accepted the diagnosis, I concluded that I could not possibly begin down the prescribed path, which would potentially end with gender reassignment surgery.

I left there not knowing what to do. I needed time to sort things out. At the time, I was not willing or able to pay the social, economic and emotional price that would be involved, not to mention the incredible impact this would have on my wife and our three sons.

The big part of my ongoing struggle is that I've always felt at odds with my body. But these confusing feelings were always kept private. Growing up, I sought to be what most defined as "normal," even as I struggled with my own gender identity. As early as the age of four, I remember becoming aware of this dynamic, I also remember sensing that I had to keep these thoughts to myself. As a child, I would often pray that I could wake up with a new body. Then, as I got older, I prayed for God to correct my brain. What research I did on my own just left me more depressed, confused and totally defeated. I begged God to make me normal, one way or another.

It wasn't until I was almost 40 that I finally sought professional help. Seeing a psychiatrist for the first time in my life was not easy. However, he skillfully helped me to verbalize my conflicting thoughts. He also offered to refer me to the Gender Clinic, but I refused. "Hell, no!" was my response. It would take me almost ten years to finally accept his recommendation and ask my GP to refer me to the clinic. Perhaps they now had a cure—that was my hope for going.

Why am I sharing all of this, and why now?

My hope is that by sharing honestly with you, you will be able to understand that it is time for me to face life honestly and allow the hidden person inside me to emerge. Like a butterfly? Maybe not quite that, but a metamorphosis nonetheless. And the new person will need to inhabit the place that has been vacated by the person you thought you knew.

As to why now, that is a harder question to answer. You can imagine the struggle I have had in reconciling this to myself and to my family. I just know that I cannot live the rest of my life attempting to maintain the shaky facade I have had to erect all my life. I trained my-self to behave and act in certain ways for more than five decades, not only for the sake of others, but as a way to survive. So there is need for a time of restructuring. Fortunately, caring professionals are helping me to navigate these intimidating waters.

I cannot express how I am feeling these days. On one hand, I have never been so scared and felt as vulnerable. On the other, I felt a very large burden finally lift from my shoulders as I began the process of disclosing. The most difficult of these, second only to disclosing to my wife more than 25 years ago (before I understood my condition), was disclosing to my parents and to each of our sons. This finally took place in the spring of 2008. I had already shared with my sisters and brother and their respective spouses a few months earlier. Though each person has accepted the news in his or her own way, I am grateful that I have not been rejected and ostracized. The complete opposite is true. I have never felt as loved and accepted.

I have also shared with close friends and clients, and that circle has been growing gradually. At first, each disclosure was emotionally exhausting. That helped to slow down the pace, though at times I wished I could have shouted it from the rooftops and gotten it over with—once and for all! Now I find that forwarding this letter to people as the need arises has made the process easier on all. It gives people a chance to absorb things at their own pace, and I am spared from having to retell things over and over again.

All of this has been very difficult for my wife, who feels as if she has lost her husband. I have felt at times that I defrauded her when I married her. My only defense is that I honestly believed that marriage was the answer to prayers for a normal gender identity. When this un-invited inner person resurfaced, I then prayed and hoped that being a father would finally do the trick. What more proof would I need? On and on, my hopes and prayers were always based on yet another milestone of manhood. In all honesty, it is really to her credit and God's grace that we have remained together since I first revealed my gender dysphoria to her.

I am eternally grateful that three sons resulted from our union. Had I been brave enough to come out sooner and not married, I may have avoided years of struggle, but then these three wonderful lives would not be here today, and I would not have known the love that I have experienced from my dear wife and our sons. This I cannot deny and I would not trade the past—even if it were possible to do so.

I am alive today because my faith enabled me to live a life that is one thing on the outside, and a very different thing on the inside—but I felt as if I had simply become a master of disguise. More importantly, my faith protected me and kept me from harmful and self-destructive behavior, which is not uncommon for individuals saddled with my condition.

I am aware that not everyone will accept my transsexualism as a genuine medical condition—as something I was born with—but rather as a lifestyle choice. I spiritualized it and tried to deal with it as though it was a matter of the will and something that could be eliminated by the retraining of my mind, by perseverance and dying to myself daily. This is what I desperately prayed for and tried to do as I struggled to reconcile my identity with my beliefs.

After all these years I have finally come to peace about my diagnosis. As my pastor put it, this is not a moral issue anymore than being born with a physical disability or any other medical condition.

But I am guilty of a sin, and that 'sin' has been my reliance on the secrecy that has underscored my adult life. It is not that I have been living a lie—but rather living without acknowledging the full truth about myself.

The Changes —

In July of 2008 I started living full time as a female. Until then, coping had been possible by a gradual discovery of what allowed me to be at peace with my body. Dressing in an attempt to present realistically as female was a learning experience, yet there were changes I had to make before I felt confident enough to be in public. For example, I have endured and will continue to endure countless hours of electrolysis to remove my entire beard and fortunately, it is almost all gone. I also needed to lose weight and was able to come close to the weight of an average female of my age and height. Finally, there was the issue of an age-appropriate wardrobe that would allow me to fly under the radar without drawing attention.

Though my physical appearance has gradually changed since I transitioned, I am still the same person inside, but I am no longer a dual person. I am no longer cloaked in silence and motivated by fear and a sense of shame from not being truthful about myself. What is new for me is that now when I am asked how I am doing, I give an honest answer and not one that is complicit with a cover-up. You don't know what a joy it is for me to now be able to answer that question honestly and to be transparent! I have nothing to hide.

The final step in the long process of transformation took place on March 30, 2010. I underwent gender reassignment surgery in Montreal. Friends asked me before the surgery if I was excited or nervous. The truth is that I was neither. What I felt was relief since I would no longer be straddling the gender divide. There is a sense of calmness that I have felt ever since and it is most welcomed.

In closing, I don't know how much you may already know or understand about transsexualism. There are many professional resources on the Internet that I can provide links to. Others continue to explain transsexualism and its ramifications better than I possibly could, but if you have questions of me, please feel free to ask. Let me know if you would like me to forward links to you because simply doing a search on the web can be quite disturbing. Unfortunately, there is much pornography based on this issue.

I have shared with you because I felt it was safe and important to do so. I apologize for not having shared with you directly and for relying on what amounts to be a "form letter." Because I value friendships, I was compelled to include you so that we can continue journeying together in complete openness.

Yours with all sincerity,
Lisa Salazar

Where did the name "Lisa" come from?

Friends have asked how I ended up with Lisa as my name. I don't really have an explanation, other than to say that it was a name I was drawn to emotionally. My brother has the following theory: He remembers that our sister Angela's nickname was "Mechilisa." It is a coined word from two Spanish words, mechas and lisa, literally meaning straight bangs. As a little girl she had straight bangs and that is what Dad called her in an endearing way. Perhaps I yearned for that kind of affection from Dad and Lisa resonates deep in my person with that yearning.

Made in the USA
Lexington, KY
16 October 2017